BROKEN
FLOWERS

A Commentary on the Tragedy of Sex Slavery in America

Pasco A. Manzo

foreword by Zollie Smith

www.runforfreedom.net

Broken Flowers
A Commentary on the Tragedy of Sex Slavery in America
by Pasco A. Manzo

COPYRIGHT © 2011 by Dream Again Ministries

Dream Again Ministries
d.b.a. Run for Freedom
P.O. Box 121122
Clermont, FL 34712

All Scripture quotations are taken from the Holy Bible, New International Version®. NIV®. Copyright © 1973, 1978, 1984 by International Bible Society, Zondervan Bible Publishers.

Cover Design and Layout Design by Tiffany McGlone
sites.google.com/site/tiffanymcglonedesign

Cover Photograph by Rachel Manzo

Back Cover Photograph by Stephen Theriault

ISBN: 978-0-615-53399-5

Printed in the United States of America
2011 - First Edition

Dedication

I dedicate this book to my wife, Mary Ann, who often reminded me how she is like a flower, which can easily be broken if not treated gently. This book is also dedicated to my daughter, Rachel, who will always be my little flower even though she has blossomed into a beautiful woman. Lastly, I dedicate this book to all the many delicate flowers, who have been broken and are in need of restoration.

Contents

Foreword

Zollie Smith
Executive Director of the
Assemblies of God U.S. Missions

The ongoing violation of inhumanity against humanity cannot and must not ever be acceptable. There is no greater atrocity against humanity than the blatant violation of the right to freedom (afforded by God and a civil society) by a fellow human being against another -- it is one of the greatest evils known to mankind and cannot be tolerated.

Pasco has been driven to write this book by his passion for those who have become victims of a world wide evil identified as Human Trafficking. I applaud him for not only his stand against this inhumane act but his desire to be actively involved in the fight to uproot it once and for all. He realizes that this is not a one-person battle but it will require the involvement of everyone. His approach is to mobilize everyone through educational awareness of this great evil and encourage all to do something to stop it.

This book is an exceptional tool that will quickly

educate and empower the reader to no longer hang out on the sidelines but to get involved in the warfare against "Modern Day Sex Slavery" because it is too close to home. Therefore, I implore you to join forces with a mighty army in the fight to eradicate this evil from amongst humanity. Together with people like Pasco and you, we can do it with God's help.

Acknowledgments

This book could not have been completed without the assistance of some amazing people.

Shelly Estes is a young lady who is concerned about the sexual exploitation of innocent girls. She is our cover's broken flower model.

Rachel Manzo is an integral part of the "One More" Chapter in Rhode Island and is a spokesperson for Run for Freedom. She enjoys photography and is responsible for the front cover photo.

Stephen Theriault is a young creative professional photographer. He took the really cool picture of Mary Ann and me that is displayed on the back cover.

Tiffany McGlone is Run for Freedom's Art and Graphics Director. She is a highly gifted graphic designer who created all the graphics, design and layout from the front cover to the back cover.

Melissa Moses and her husband are our neighbors and monthly partners. She had to wade through some disturbing information while conducting her research.

Mary Ann Manzo, co-founder of Run For Freedom, has played a significant role investing many hours on sentence structure.

Rosalie LaPinto teaches English Composition to college freshmen and after hearing me speak in her local church she offered her help and made valuable suggestions.

Isaac Manzo is an attorney in Orlando, Florida and has an exceptionally keen mind for critical analysis. He constructively pointed out some issues that needed to be addressed.

Marla Castrilli is a bright young girl who has a burden for victims of sex trafficking and also serves as our Executive Assistant. She diligently categorized all the endnotes.

Ed Russo is an incredible man of God who cares about young people entrapped in the sex industry. It was his inspiration that caused me to write about the value of pennies in Chapter 7.

Special Thanks to those who took time to read and critique the manuscript. **Lynda Giarrusso, Deborah**

McDonald, Jesse Maley, Arthur Ricci III, and Joan Sullivan.

Dream Again Ministries Board, Run for Freedom Staff, "One More" Chapters, Volunteers, and our faithful Monthly Financial Partners for their continual support and belief that we can win this fight against Sex Slavery.

I would be remiss if I did not acknowledge and thank the One Who breathes life into me, Who sustains me daily, Who fills me with His love. It is *Jesus* Who gives me the passion and strength to help restore *broken flowers*.

A Note to the Reader

Reading this book can change you, and, in turn, you can help change America's outlook on Sex Slavery! I know there are more qualified and gifted people who write books, but I plunged into this endeavor due to my burning passion for those who have been victimized and exploited.

Although there are a broad range of abuses that fall under the category of Human Trafficking, including, but not limited to, crimes against young men, young women, and children, and everything from domestic servitude to commercial sex to the harvesting of human organs, this book focuses primarily on Sex Slavery as it affects young women.

Any similarity between Run for Freedom's use of the color orange to represent freedom, and the use of the color orange by any political, religious, or ethnic cause, is purely coincidental, and should not be taken as an endorsement by the author of any particular political, religious, or ethnic cause.

Names have been changed to maintain the anonymity of the people referred in this book.

I have spoken publicly to a wide variety of

audiences hundreds of times to raise awareness of Sex Slavery. These groups include churches, Rotary and Lions Clubs, law enforcement organizations, judges, bankers, mens, youth and young adults. I have also had the opportunity to appear on television and radio talk shows, and have given magazine and newspaper interviews. When given the opportunity, I usually ask my audiences the following questions:

- How many know the National Hotline Number to report a suspected victim of Human Trafficking (888-3737-888)?
- How many know the date of the National Human Trafficking Awareness Day (January 11th)?

No one ever knows the answers.

Out of three hundred eleven million Americans I believe less than one percent can articulate with clarity the problem of Sex Slavery in America.[1]

The idea is for you to be different after you have read this book. Hopefully, informed, influenced, and inspired! It is my desire that you will have a much deeper understanding of the covert dealings of Sex Slavery, and that you will be challenged to make a difference.

The key to eradicating Sex Slavery in America is AWARENESS, AWARENESS, and more AWARENESS! Creating that awareness is a huge challenge for Run for Freedom and other organizations that are fighting this battle.

We can establish Dream Homes, treatment centers, and safe places, which can offer medicine, psychological counseling, and equine therapy; we can petition for stiffer laws and penalties against the criminals; but without raising awareness at every level of society, there will be no significant change.

I have two objectives in publishing this book: first, to raise awareness of Sex Slavery in America. Second, to inspire you to enlist in this ever-growing army that is fighting to free those who have become sex slaves in America.

The proceeds from the sale of this book will go towards the eradication of Sex Slavery in America.

Introduction

What follows here is a brief but disturbingly accurate explanation of Human Trafficking and Sex Slavery.

What is Human Trafficking?

Human Trafficking is defined in the Trafficking in Persons Protocol adopted by the United Nations as "the recruitment, transport, transfer, harboring and receiving of a person by such means as threat or use of force or other forms of coercion, of abduction of fraud or deception for the purpose of exploitation." [1]

> Human Trafficking is a crime against humanity, but even more significantly it is a crime against the laws of God.

Every year, thousands of men, women, and children fall into the hands of traffickers, and every country in the world is affected by serving as either a country of origin, transit, or destination for the victims.

Human Trafficking is the illegal trade in human beings for the purposes of commercial sexual exploitation, forced labor and organ harvesting. It is a modern-day adaptation of slavery. It is – without question – the fastest growing criminal industry in the world. [2]

Human Trafficking includes twenty-seven million slaves (sex and labor) in the world today; eight hundred thousand are being trafficked annually. The misconception is that trafficking only takes place overseas.

However, in the United States, it is estimated that 18,000 to 24,000 persons are trafficked annually. [3]

Human Trafficking is often thought of as only a crime of movement of people. But it is not *primarily* a crime of movement, even though people are moved from place to place, city to city, state to state, and from country to country. Once you look beneath the surface you will discover it is a crime that *exploits* innocent people. [4]

The Fundamentals of Human Trafficking

What is trafficking of people?

Recruitment, transportation, transferring, harboring or receiving of persons.

How are people trafficked?

Through kidnapping, threat, force, coercion, fraud, deception, abuse of power or vulnerability, or by giving payments or benefits to a person in control of the victim.

Who are the people trafficked?

Men and women, boys and girls, of all ages from all classes, all ethnicities, and all backgrounds. Statistically, 60% of traffickers are actually females who were formerly trafficked victims themselves. [5]

Why are people trafficked?

For the purpose of exploitation, which includes prostitution, sexual exploitation; servitude, which is forced labor; or for slavery or similar practices. There is even a growing industry in the forced removal and trafficking of human organs. Financial gain is at the center of all these hideous crimes.

"For the love of money is a root of all kinds of evil." (1 Timothy 6:10).

What is Sex Slavery?

Sex Slavery is a person or persons being forced, coerced, blackmailed and/or manipulated into being involved in a myriad of sexual practices with another person or persons. It can be a single owner of one or two or a highly organized network of many.

Sex Slavery is often thought of as a crime about sex, but it is more than the deviant preferences and practices of people. It is less about sensual desire and physical pleasure than it is about barbaric people consumed with greed, who care more about personal gain than people made in the image of God. [6]

How are people enslaved?

No one wakes up and says, "I am going to become a sex slave today." They are entrapped in numerous ways by highly organized crime, street pimps or perhaps even someone in the neighborhood. Sex advertisements are placed in newspapers and online. Misinformed parents send their children off to escape poverty. Some modeling and dating agencies are fronts for recruitment. Clients may be told up front they will be working in the sex industry – such as at a strip club, escort service or a pornography studio – never imagining they will end up sex slaves.

Who could be a victim of Sex Slavery?

It could be an eight-year-old girl who is sold by her single mother right in her own home. It could be a twenty-one-year-old girl who is forced to have sex with her boyfriend's friends. It could be a wife, manipulated by her husband to sell her body. It could be a runaway teenager who is promised a better situation by a pimp. It could be someone who responds to a phony job advertisement for modeling, waitressing or acting. It could be someone who accepts a false bridal proposal only to be sold to a sex trafficker. It could be... *almost anyone you know.*

Victims of Sex Slavery are people of both genders, as well as people of all sexual orientations, ages, races, ethnicities, and religions. A victim can be *anyone*, who comes from *any* neighborhood, or *any* class of citizens. Yet, some people are more vulnerable due to being homeless, unaware, uneducated, unemployed, victims of poverty or political instability, or in financial debt.

It could be your daughter, your wife, your sister or your friend. No one is immune to the dedicated trafficker who is constantly on the prowl for "new recruits" for his or her business.

Why do victims not run for their freedom?

Traffickers are masters at using various techniques to instill fear and dependency in their victims to keep them enslaved. The most frequently used techniques include, but are in no way limited to: [7]

- Drug Addiction: The victim is introduced to drugs by traffickers and becomes dependent on the drug to fulfill the sexual requirements of the client.
- Debt Bondage: The victim has never ending

financial obligations that are impossible to eradicate.

- Isolation: The victim's contact with the public is fully monitored or completely denied.
- Confiscation: The victim's personal identification documents are removed from their possession.
- Threats: The victim lives in fear of imprisonment, deportation, and/or harm to family members.
- Violence: The victim endures sexual, emotional, physical, and verbal abuse.

The Stockholm Syndrome, also known as trauma bonding is commonplace among victims of Sex Slavery. This phenomenon, whereby the victim has sympathetic feelings of concern or love toward the trafficker, is almost always a factor in the victim's failing to run for freedom, even when the opportunity arises repeatedly.

It is a small wonder that women who have been sex trafficked almost unanimously report symptoms of Post Traumatic Stress Disorder. [8]

Are victims trafficked into the United States?

Yes, victims enter the U.S. both legally with

proper documentation and illegally with false or no documentation. [9]

What can be done to end Sex Slavery in America?

Awareness that reaches every sphere of society can *eradicate* Sex Slavery in America. It will take an army of passionate people fervently fighting against this atrocity.

My wife Mary Ann and I, along with other Run for Freedom staff, financial partners, volunteers, our "One More" chapters; and a small army of devoted and passionate people are responding to that call. We have committed our lives to raise awareness of Sex Slavery across America using all available means.

We feel deep compassion for these *broken flowers*, who have been victimized by greedy and cruel individuals who have forced, deceived, and held them captive against their will, selling them daily into prostitution. We are dedicated to offering them recovery and restoration – physically, psychologically, emotionally and spiritually – by any means necessary through the strength of a God whose heart breaks for these "lives interrupted."

Our Christian values oblige us to seek freedom for these *broken flowers*. We will educate, inform, and challenge the powers that be to help us eradicate Sex Slavery.

How about you? Will you join this army? Abraham Lincoln, the 16th President of the United States (1861-1865), who brought about the emancipation of American slaves, encouraged his fellow Americans with passion in his heart when he proclaimed to the people, *"To sin by silence – when they should protest - makes cowards of men."*

1 The Origin of Sex Slavery in America

Being a good old American boy...wait a minute let me back up a bit. I wasn't always such a good boy. My younger days were full of making wrong choices. You know, stealing, sleeping around, abusing drugs, gambling, selling black market contraband, and making fast money.

I grew up in a day when the neighborhood kids had a "wannabe" gangster mentality. The infamous Al Capone and other local mob bosses were our idols. We understood that in the criminal world it was all about power and money. Whatever it took to get "there," they did it.

Interestingly, the upper echelons of organized crime had a loosely based code of ethics. They could go to church, pray over a meal, while simultaneously ordering a hit on someone who would wind up in the trunk of a car with a bullet in their head or at the bottom of an ocean with cement shoes.

Some discriminating gangsters would never smuggle or sell drugs, considering it evil, while others saw the profit potential but only allowed their distribution in neighborhoods other than their own; and then there were others who didn't care who or how many people overdosed in a day.

Nightclubs, bars, lounges, restaurants, and casinos were just some of the mob owned and operated businesses. Some of these guys we wanted to emulate as kids would be faithful to their wives, while others had no boundaries when it came to the number of sex partners they had.

As much as I knew about the criminal world growing up, I did not know about Sex Slavery. I did not know about the young girls that were forced to have sex several times a day to turn profits for their owners. I did not know how lucrative selling sex could be. I did not know how heartbreaking and emotionally damaging this was for the young girls who had been sexually victimized. I did not know that the first record

– although certainly not the first instance – of a girl trafficked for sexual exploitation from Europe into the United States happened in 1861[1] and that it has not stopped even up to the writing of this book.

> I did not know that these girls were *broken flowers* that nobody seemed to know or care about.

It is hard to imagine, but in the early 1900s the atrocity of trafficking and selling American and foreign girls for the purpose of Sex Slavery was so prevalent that in 1913 Universal Pictures produced a silent film titled *Traffic in Souls*. Let me tell you how I stumbled on it.

As I was writing this chapter and visiting with my daughter one night, we decided to watch a movie. As she was searching the Turner Classic Movie channel, she found *Traffic in Souls*, described as, "a 1913 silent film about white Sex Slavery in America."

Surprised, and finding it hard to believe that such a movie would be produced in that era when so few movies were even made, we watched the scratchy Kinescope melodrama. As we read the script boards, we were transported back in time to America's early 1900s. Directed by George Loane Tucker at a cost of $25,000, the movie depicts how girls were kidnapped and forced into prostitution. The storyline accurately portrays a criminal sex slave ring that kidnaps young female immigrants arriving at Ellis Island, New York, as well as local American girls, and forces them into prostitution.

The movie dramatizes a scenario where a European ship comes to New York, and a recruiter scouts out a pair of blond-haired Swedish sisters. He uses the newest technology of the day – a wireless telegraph – to radio ahead so the con man will take his position. Another story is of a housewife who is deceitfully lured off the streets and brought to a house of prostitution.

The central story is of a male agent of the Sex Slavery organization who sees the vulnerable Lorna on the job at a candy store and pretends to be interested in her hand in marriage. He takes her out on a date, drugs her, and sells her into prostitution through a bogus employment agency.

After Lorna disappears, her sister Mary appeals frantically to her own fiancé. He happens to be a heroic New York policeman who has become suspicious of the operation and has already been involved in rescuing victims from a house of prostitution. Mary ultimately loses her job at the candy store because of her sister's shame. She takes a new job as a secretary working undercover for the feigned "Purity and Reform League" and discovers that her fiancé was right to be suspicious. It is really a front used to launder the huge amount of money coming in from the prostitution ring.

The movie takes a surprising turn when it is discovered that the boss – Mr. Trubus – who is running the feigned employment operation, is none other than the Reform League President. He is part of high society, wealthy and respected in the community. While committing this horrible crime against New York's innocent girls, Trubus is preparing for his own daughter's marriage. Mary enlists the help of her invalid but technologically gifted father, Isaac, who ultimately invents a device that will transfer dictograph conversations to a phonograph. Trubus' conversations are recorded as evidence, and the police march out for the bust. Trubus, the ringleader is arrested and the wedding plans are cancelled.

> *Traffic in Souls* shows us that white Sex Slavery was prominent enough in the late 1800s and early 1900s that a sensational movie was produced to expose it.

This film ran 76 minutes on six reels; it was one of the American film industry's most expensive epic productions of its time and helped launch Universal Pictures. It was a huge box office success. This controversial film grossed a half million dollars when movie tickets cost just a quarter! Two million people saw this movie during a time when people did not even say the word "sex" in anything other than a whisper and behind closed doors! [2]

The white slave trade has been glamorized in the popular 2010 HBO series, *Boardwalk Empire*, recounting in part the activities of Maurice Van Bever who worked in collusion with Chicago mobster Big Jim Colosimo. In the early 1900s, Van Bever devised a code used in letters and telegrams to warn the traffickers of danger.

Big Jim's white slave gang prospered for more than six years. He imported hundreds of young girls to Chicago, had them "broken in" by professional rapists, and sold them to brothel keepers for anywhere from $10 to $150. One fifteen-year-old girl managed to escape through the window of a brothel and run for her freedom to the police station. Here's an excerpt of her report, courtesy of Herbert Asbury's classic *Gem of the Prairie*:

"My home is in Milwaukee. Some time ago I met a nice-appearing young man from Chicago in Milwaukee. He seemed interested in me and I thought he was honorable. He promised to get me a nice position in Chicago at eight dollars a week if I would come down here, and I came. I knew nothing about Chicago. He took me straight to the house at 2115 Armour Avenue, and as soon as I entered the place I knew something was wrong. But I saw there was no chance to get away. My

street clothes were taken away from me, and there was nothing for me to do but to submit to orders."

The brothel keeper's lawyers, hired by Big Jim and Van Bever, subpoenaed dozens of witnesses, all of whom testified that the girl's character was very bad; "so bad," as the *Record Herald* put it, "that the stainless joint keeper had rendered her almost a service by allowing her to live in his establishments." The jury found the brothel keeper not guilty.

Operations of the Big Jim and the Van Bever gang were momentarily stalled in 1909, when federal agents gathered evidence about a dozen young prostitutes who had been sent from St. Louis to Chicago. Van Bever, his madam wife, and several other members of the gang were each fined a thousand dollars and sentenced to one year in prison. But Big Jim's clout was such that, in the words of the official report, "he could not be reached."

A woman who heard me speak on "Human

Trafficking Breaks the Heart of God," gave me a historic, informative and zealous book entitled, *The Great War on White Slavery* or *Fighting for the Protection of Our Girls*, written by Clifford G. Roe in 1911. It details tragic events that surrounded the cruel, lucrative business of the early 1900s, known as "white sex slavery." B.S. Steadwell's review states, "This book was the official weapon in this Great Crusade [against white slavery]." [3]

The following information is drawn from Roe's book, beginning with his introduction, which contains these snippets:

"Truthful and chaste account of the hideous trade of buying and selling young girls for immoral purpose. Startling disclosures made by white slaves during the trials of many procurers and traders. The cruel and inhuman treatment of white slaves. Graphic accounts of how white slaves are ensnared and a full exposition of the methods and schemes used to lure and trap the girls."

Roe explains,

"Early on, the girl slave trade was carried on by the sale of girls from Eastern Europe into the Orient through the distributing center in Constantinople.

The victims of this traffic were recruited chiefly from the ghettos of Europe in the old Kingdom of Poland, now a part of Russia and Austria. The kaftan, as the procurer was then called, gathered up the girls in Galicia, Russia, and Poland and sold them into Asia.

"It was the traffickers in France who first developed the business of exploiting girls to supply the prostitution resorts of North America. Many of these girls were lured with promises of marriage and securing work.

"French girl slaves soon became common in New York, Chicago, San Francisco, and other American cities. In New York City those who developed this traffic were known as Cadets. The crowded conditions on the East Side of New York gave these Cadets a great field in which to work. Corrupt politicians in New York City, anxious to control the districts largely populated by foreigners, winked at the sale of girls by the Cadets and sometimes even aided in it.

"Traffickers were selling girls for $50 when most working people were making $18 a month and

$200 a year.

"Proof came through the United States courts early in the 1900s by sworn testimony given before the grand jury. By a special act of Congress, on February 20, 1907, a commission was created consisting of three Senators, three members of the House of Representatives, and three persons appointed by the President of the United States to make a full inquiry into the subject of the traffic of girls and the immigration issues tied to it.

"Clarence Gentry was found guilty of trafficking women and children and was sentenced on January 28, 1910 to serve six months in jail and pay a paltry fine of three hundred dollars.

"From the Atlantic to the Pacific the abominable traffic in girls can be found. Harry Levinson of New York City, on May 2, 1910, was indicted for pandering two girls to agents of the White Slavery Grand Jury. He told how he procured girls and how white slavery agents were constantly at work finding girls for houses of ill fame. It was their business to engage attractive young girls in conversation, take them out to dinner, and paint a dazzling picture of

the life of luxury they might lead.

"Paul Sinclair, a reformed trafficker had been one of the cleverest procurers operating in the United States. Paul did not appear to be a villainous individual, as one might think. No, he was a quiet, mild mannered young man. He would place advertisements in the paper that read:

WANTED: Lady partner for vaudeville sketch, one who can sing and play piano preferred. Must have good appearance. Will furnish wardrobe for stage and street.

WANTED: Chorus girls for a burlesque company. Good pay and promotion for those willing to work, experience unnecessary.

"Paul's going rate for selling a girl was $50, which was then credited to her debt account. When the girls were brought in they were always put in debt to the house and had to stay there and work it off.

Transportation was added to the money paid the trafficker, and the madam would buy house clothes for the girl. They had to pay board or rent. Girls very seldom got out of debt.

"The house would pay a doctor to examine the girls once a week and then add that cost to the girls' indenture. During this era, social hygiene was limited and syphilis posed a great danger with little known about preventing or treating it. Prostitutes who contracted the disease were put out on the street to die. The girls would be instructed how to answer police officers who came looking for them. Some were as young as sixteen. They were allowed one day off a week but never alone, and they couldn't talk to strangers.

"If the traffickers thought there was anyone who called to see the same girl too often and that he might try to take her away, he would not be allowed in the place again.

"Traffickers would beat the girls so that they would not be able to get out of bed for a week. Sometimes it would be for not making enough money, other times for daring to be sick.

"All the large American cities have become trading centers for the girl slave agents. No one race or creed predominates in this awful business. Even a former schoolteacher, Dora Douglas, was convicted and sentenced to prison in Chicago in December of 1908, for procuring girls from Milwaukee, Wisconsin.

"Everywhere, girls are being hunted like animals. It may be a country fair, a street carnival, at the public dance, on excursion boats, in summer parks, nickel theatres, in waiting rooms, in stores, or walking home from school. The trafficker stops at nothing, not even at church. Hundreds of times he has been known to track his quarry after prayer meeting, marry her with much village pomp, and sell her into a den of infamy during her "honeymoon." Her clothes are locked away; and she is drugged, or made intoxicated to gain control.

"A procurer is ever on the watch for these new victims. He dresses well and has a certain polished manner, which impresses inexperienced girls deeply. At carnivals, pickpockets, sneak thieves, fakers, and confidence men are all out in full force.

Panders do not always work singly; quite often they work in teams, often with a woman in tow to inspire authenticity.

"Even public officials and employees of large business concerns and corporations have been enticed by the lure of gold to assist and aid those who deal in the white sex slave market.

"More than a thousand cases had come to public notice in the United States in the year 1910 where traffickers were indicted under the White Slave Act.

"Who would have ever prophesied a century ago that today the daughters of people would be bought and sold like hardware and groceries? It will never be blotted out until we change social conditions, educate men to a higher standard of right and wrong, and wipe out the demand for sex slaves. There will be commercialized vice as long as men demand it and women can be found to supply it.

"White slavery is the outgrowth of an over stimulated demand, incited and encouraged by men and women, low and degenerate, grasping and avaricious, greedy for money; no demand, no supply!

"White Slavers carry on their business so quietly and shrewdly that prosecution and conviction is almost impossible even under the most favorable conditions. Reports in the public prints detail conditions of the most brutal depravity. Children held in the slavery of vice by human monsters and perhaps murder committed to conceal other infamous offences. So long as it exists corrupt men will continue to profit by the practice.

"The males have absolutely no moral standard, thinking of nothing but the money that may be made. They by no means pause to consider the means by which it is made, and they look upon the female simply the way a merchant regards his assets.

"It is my judgment that the only cure for this evil is that they be hounded as they deserve to be, or hanged. They are inhuman; they have become beastly, and unfit to live in a community of human beings. No legislation, however drastic, can be too *severe to punish these malefactors."*

Roe's book might be dated over a hundred years ago, but it references the same deceptive methods that are used to lure girls today. He also gives the same advice for prevention that needs to be heard and heeded again. It is still all about the money!

Unfortunately, the penalties for such terrible crimes were no more than a slap on the wrist a century ago, and not much has changed in a hundred years.

Today, the average "shelf life" of an adolescent girl forced into Sex Slavery is seven years. These girls live a horrible life of shame, pain, disease and low self-esteem. Some escape and then return because they find that they cannot escape the damage done to them and the stigma that is forever attached to their names. Others are rescued and restored; but whatever the cause of their departure from this miserable life, the ultimate outcome is always the same. For every girl that escapes, another victim is required to take her place.[4]

In 1910, at least 60,000 new girls and women were required every year – 5,000 every month – to provide for the constant demand of the public houses of prostitution.[5] In 2010, the *Broward-Palm Beach New Times Newspaper* wrote, "as many as 100,000 prostitutes -- male and female -- will descend upon South Florida in hopes of cashing in with football fans before the Miami Super Bowl XXXIII." [6]

Sex Slavery is not a "private evil" but a public business. It is a commercialized institution, and its incentive is not only lust but also greed.

The traffic in girls for sexual exploitation relies upon the secrecy of its operations, and its inherent filthiness often protects it from open consideration and public discussion. Run for Freedom is committed to exposing this atrocity through every possible means.

To remain silent is an offense. America is ready for the eradication of this crime that is victimizing innocent young people.

We need the moral conscience of every person to be aroused, and for good people to fight against those who are exploiting sex slave victims. This responsibility needs to be assumed by every man and woman in America.

Edmund Burke said, "For evil to prevail good men [and women] just need to do nothing." Someone else has said, "If you aren't part of the solution, then you are part of the problem!"

You may feel that this does not concern you, but it does. It is the responsibility of every person to look out for someone else's daughter and protect her moral purity as eagerly as that of his or her own child.

Together we can fight to eradicate Sex Slavery and remove this slimy evil from the social fabric of America.

Prostitution: Good or Evil?

Prostitution has several definitions attached to it, but the simplest and most common is, *the act of offering one's self for hire to engage in sexual relations.* Payment typically received is in the form of cash or goods.

Prostitution is sometimes referred to as the "world's oldest profession." It is listed among the crimes some refer to as victimless or consensual crimes because no one present at the crime is unwilling. When one looks more deeply, however, research shows that in most cases this is not the true picture of prostitution.

Types of Prostitution

A variety of terms are used for those who engage in prostitution, some distinguish between different kinds of prostitutes, or imply the type of service performed.

Prostitute is the most generally accepted term. The common alternative word is *whore.*

The English word **whore** derives from the Old English word hōra, from the Indo-European root kā meaning, "desire". Use of the word *whore* is widely considered derogatory, especially in its modern slang form of "ho".

An **escort** or **call girl** makes appointments by phone. You can usually find them in the *Yellow Pages*, newspapers, and magazines or on the Internet. The act takes place at the customer's place of residence or more commonly at his hotel room (referred to as *out-call*), or at the escort's place of residence or in a hotel room rented for the occasion by the escort (*in-call*). This form of prostitution is often sheltered under the umbrella of escort agencies that ostensibly supply attractive escorts for social occasions. While escort agencies claim never to provide sexual services, very few successful escorts are available exclusively for social companionship. While the escort agency is paid a fee for this booking and dispatch service, the customer must usually negotiate an additional fee for any sex related services. Even where this type of prostitution is legal, the ambiguous term escort service is commonly used. Not all professional escorts are prostitutes.

Hookers or **street prostitutes** solicit customers by waiting on a street corner or by walking the streets; the setting is in public places. Their pimps or madams are usually in close range to monitor all actions and transactions. The prostitutes usually dress in skimpy, provocative clothing, regardless of the weather. Servicing the customers is described as "turning tricks." The sex is performed in the customer's car, in a nearby alley, or in a rented room. Motels and hotels which accommodate prostitutes commonly rent rooms by the half or full hour.

An **online prostitute** uses websites that offer their clientele the ability to post sex advertisements. Adult boards will have contact details, such as email addresses, local addresses, and prices. The customer will make the transactions and meet up with the prostitute. Also online are adult contact sites, chats and communities. There are thousands of websites viewed where services are purchased while individuals maintain their anonymity. The majority of the time the sex worker is being *prostituted*, and her owner places the advertisements on the site.

Some tech-savvy pimps use social networking websites to recruit underage girls.

According to Ernie Allen, president and CEO of the National Center for Missing and Exploited Children, or NCMEC, the Internet has given pimps the ability to recruit young girls not just from poor, broken homes, but from a broad spectrum of society. [1]

A **brothel** also known as a **cathouse, whorehouse, sporting house,** as well as by other names, is an establishment dedicated to prostitution, providing the prostitutes a place to meet and to have sex with clients. Often these are found in red-light districts in cities across America.

A **massage parlor** or **spa** located in professional settings. The massage involves the client being treated while lying on a massage table, sitting in a massage chair or lying on a mat on the floor. The massage subject may be fully or partly unclothed. Parts of the body may be covered with towels or sheets. Those who practice massage as a career are referred to as massage therapists. In many of these establishments across America illegal sex acts are being performed.

A **strip club**, or **gentleman's club** is an adult entertainment venue in which striptease, lap dancing, or exotic dance (topless or fully nude), is performed regularly. Strip clubs typically adopt a nightclub or bar style, but can also adopt a theater or cabaret style. Because they promote sexual desire, lust, and lasciviousness, many clubs have a variety of other layers of sexual activity available for an additional cost.

Phone sex workers provide a type of virtual sex. It refers to sexually explicit conversation between two or more persons via telephone. Often at least one of the participants masturbates or engages in sexual fantasy. Phone sex conversation may include (but not limited to) guided sexual sounds, narrated and enacted suggestions; sexual anecdotes and confessions; and candid expression of sexual feelings, all for a price and oftentimes at the expense of someone's personal freedom.

A *lot lizard* mainly serves those in the trucking industry at truck stops and shopping centers. Prostitutes will often proposition male truckers using a CB radio from a vehicle parked in the non-commercial section of a truck stop parking lot, communicating through codes based on commercial driving slang, then joining the driver in his truck.

Commercial sex worker (CSW) or *sex trade worker* (STW) are terms often used for those seeking to remove the social stigma associated with prostitution. In many cases these workers are prostituted, forced, threatened, coerced, and/or deceived into performing sexual acts and receive little to no money or goods for their services.

Organizers of prostitution are typically known as *pimps* (if male) and *madams* (if female). A *sex trafficker* has a broader definition that can include organized crime. More formally, because they practice procuring, they are known as procurers or procuresses.

Commonly, pimps target girls who appear to be naive, lonely, homeless, or rebellious.

Pimps feign affection and attention to convince targets that they are "special". Then they are kept captive by verbal abuse, often referred to as a bitch, making them feel that they are worthless. They use coercion through beatings and threats. It is estimated that the majority of prostitution is pimp-controlled.

The customers of prostitutes are known as **johns** or **tricks** in America. These slang terms are used among both prostitutes and law enforcement for persons who solicit prostitutes. The term john may have originated from the customer practice of giving their name as "John," a common name in English-speaking countries, in an effort to maintain anonymity. In some places, men who drive around red-light districts for the purpose of soliciting prostitutes are also known as curb crawlers.

There are several dangers associated with the lives of prostitutes and sex slaves.

The client picks up a street prostitute and drives away with her in his car. Under these conditions she is at risk of serious abuse. Although prevalent in the late 1990s, this type of service has been steadily declining in recent years.

Prostitutes are often raped, beaten, harassed, tortured; verbally, physically and emotionally abused; have her life threatened; infected with disease, addicted to drugs, and stolen from (in order to make up the difference she has to work longer and harder).

As a result she will have long-term psychological effects such as fear, loss of freedom, suicidal thoughts and attempts (hospitals report 15% of all completed suicides are prostituted women).[2] Most prostitutes will suffer from Post Traumatic Stress Disorder (PTSD), a psychological reaction to extreme physical and emotional trauma. Symptoms include acute anxiety, depression, insomnia, irritability, flashbacks, and nightmares, emotional numbing, and being in a state of emotional and physical hyper-alertness.

A prostitute can also face death. The Craigslist Killer, Philip Markoff, a medical student at Boston University, committed first-degree murder of a masseuse who advertised her services on Craigslist. A serial killer is still at large in Long Island, New York. Police believe he may be responsible for the death of over twelve prostitutes. The Riverside, California Prostitute Killer took the lives of three women. Six decomposed bodies of prostitutes were found in Cleveland, Ohio at the home of a convicted rapist who was subsequently arrested. A motel located on the local city strip was a frequent hangout and workplace for many of the forty-eight prostitutes that fell victim to the Green River Killer. [3]

Prostitution has no age boundaries.

In ancient Rome, as the Empire grew, prostitutes were often foreign slaves, captured, purchased, or raised for that purpose, sometimes by large-scale "prostitute farmers" who peddled abandoned children. [4]

In modern America it is not much different. The National Center for Missing and Exploited Children says each year there are 450,000 children on America's streets. The data shows 100,000 to 293,000 children have become at risk or sexual commodities, with the average age being thirteen-years-old. [5]

"Prostitution is good for society." The following views are **not** the opinion of the author!

> Prostitution has been accepted, tolerated, and seen as good for society for centuries.

In the Bible Genesis 38 describes its existence and tolerance, as depicted in the story of Judah and his widowed daughter-in-law, Tamar, who posed as a prostitute at the side of the city road. Judah hired her at the high price of a young goat.

It is widely known that during the Middle Ages prostitution was commonly found in cities, although all forms of sexual activity outside of marriage was regarded as sinful by the Roman Catholic Church. Prostitution was tolerated at that time, however, because it was believed to prevent the greater evils of rape, sodomy, and masturbation. Prostitution in the middle-ages was not forced prostitution as we know today. [6]

Augustine of Hippo held that: "If you expel prostitution from society, you will unsettle everything on account of lusts." The general tolerance of prostitution was for the most part reluctant, and many urged prostitutes to reform. [7]

Groups that are fighting for decriminalization of prostitution believe that the role of prostitution is vital in our society. They believe that the largest risks are not ghastly clients or sexually transmitted diseases but the taxpayer's money being wasted by police fighting this *"crime" with no victims.*

They insist that all adults have the right to engage in consensual adult sex and that it is criminal and against the Constitution to rob adults of the freedom to do what they want to do with their bodies. They stress their point by saying all the rest of the world realizes this and that America is one of the few countries where private sex work is illegal.

It is thought that prostitutes create a safer environment for other women because men with a strong sex drive have an alternative. Those who are married but not sexually satisfied might prefer an experienced prostitute.

Some fathers are homophobic and would dread hearing the news that their son is homosexual, so at puberty they take their young sons to a prostitute so they may discover the pleasure of a woman.

It is also argued that if prostitution were regulated and decriminalized, diseases would decrease. They further argue that prostitution is legal in many other countries. [8]

In the early part of the twentieth-century prostitution was legal in the United States. Then, because of rampant white sex slavery, it became illegal in almost all states. The influence of the Women's Christian Temperance Union played a significant role in this, as well as in the banning of drug use, and was a major force in the prohibition of alcohol. [9]

Prostitution was legal in Alaska until 1953 (when it was not yet a U.S. state), and is still legal in some ten rural counties of Nevada. A legal loophole in Rhode Island decriminalized prostitution in 1980, when the laws were amended to reduce the act from a felony to a misdemeanor. The amendments left only street solicitation as illegal and, essentially, indoor prostitution not subject to prosecution. This loophole was closed in Rhode Island in 2009. [10]

The legality of prostitution and the social attitude towards it vary considerably, from being perfectly legal and seen as a job like any other job, to being considered a form of sexual exploitation of women, and to being considered an immoral act.

Laws should be changed to penalize the pimps and johns rather than the girls forced into prostitution. Victims need to be rehabilitated, not imprisoned.

Prostitution is seen as an evil in society.

There has to be a clear understanding that the majority of prostitution whether on the streets, online, in a massage parlor, through an escort service, or wherever, is forced, meaning that young women are being prostituted. In these cases either no money or very little money is actually for the personal use of the prostituted girl. They are often sold repeatedly and trafficked from state to state. The industry has created a big demand for younger girls because of the clients' sexual preference and because of a decrease in the likelihood of disease.

Huge amounts of money are laundered, and the law is constantly being broken by forced prostitution. Often the young women are arrested rather than the pimps/traffickers and clients. They are repeatedly devalued, abused, raped, and even murdered. In some cases, when they are no longer healthy, and too emotionally drained to perform sexually, their vital organs are harvested and sold. They are seen as no more than a commodity, human merchandise that is repeatedly sold for profit. It is all about the money, and it is Sex Slavery! John 3:16 says, "For God so loved the world that he gave his one and only Son, that whoever believes in him shall not perish but have eternal life." God values every person.

One of the most serious problems associated with prostitution is the fact that the sex trade is surrounded by illegal, abusive, and dangerous activities. Legalizing and regulating prostitution would not improve this problem; it would only worsen it and increase the criminal activity. Pimps could still control women working in licensed brothels. Legalizing prostitution would make it more socially acceptable to buy sex, creating a greater demand for prostitutes (both by local men and by foreigners engaging in sex tourism) and, as a result, human trafficking and underage sexual exploitation would increase in order to satisfy this demand.[11] This would also continue to increase sexually transmitted diseases. The Centers for Disease Control and Prevention notes that there are fifty known and recognized STDs of which some are incurable and fatal.

Female prostitutes are at risk of violent crime, as well as at higher risk of occupational mortality than any other group of women ever studied. [12]

The unidentified serial killer (or killers) known as Jack the Ripper is said to have killed at least five prostitutes in London in 1888. More recently, Robert Pickton, a Canadian, made headlines after the remains of twenty-six missing prostitutes were found buried on his farm. The previously mentioned "Green River Killer", Gary Ridgway, confessed to killing forty-eight prostitutes from 1982 to 1998, making him one of the most prolific serial killers in American history. [13]

Melissa Farley's study of 854 prostitutes in nine countries, including America, found that 95% of the women had been physically assaulted, 75% had been raped, and 89% stated that they wanted to leave prostitution. However, many people in prostitution are unable to leave because they are under the control of a third party (a pimp, or a controlling partner or family member). [14]

Premature death is foremost among the health risks of prostitution. In a recent United States study of almost 2,000 prostitutes followed over a 30-year period, the most common causes of death were homicide, suicide, drug and alcohol related problems, HIV infection, and accidents, in that order. The homicide rate among active female prostitutes was 17 times higher than that of the age-matched general population. [15]

The severity of Post Traumatic Stress Disorder symptoms of participants in this study was in the same range as treatment-seeking combat veterans, battered women seeking shelter, rape survivors, and refugees from state-organized torture. [16]

In a 2008 study of Chicago street prostitutes, economists Steven D. Levitt and Sudhir Alladi Venkatesh found that prostitutes are arrested once for every 450 tricks, and every tenth arrest results in jail time. Once every 30 tricks, a prostitute gives free sex to an on-duty police officer to avoid arrest. They also found that condoms are rarely used. [17]

The pimp business has an internal structure for

dealing with rule breakers built around violence. For example, pimps have been known to employ a "pimp stick," which is two coat hangers wrapped together, in order to subdue unruly prostitutes.[18] A variation is a "pimp cane," a cane used for similar purposes.

Another punishment for unruly prostitutes is to "trunk" them, whereby the pimp locks the prostitute in the trunk of a car. A prostitute could be punished for merely looking at another pimp; this is considered "reckless eyeballing." [19]

There is also a widespread practice among many pimps of tattooing as a mark of "ownership" and as a means to humiliate and dehumanize their prostitutes. [20] The mark might be as discreet as an ankle tattoo, or as blatant as a neck tattoo or a large scale font across the prostitute's lower back, thigh, chest, or buttocks. [21]

Prostitution must be differentiated from someone who is being prostituted. If you see prostitution as a consensual act, please reconsider. The prostitute, in most cases, is forced to perform. Prostitution is often about male dominance over women, reinforcing archaic stereotypical views about women as sex objects used and abused by men. Galatians 3:28 says, "There is neither Jew nor Gentile, neither slave nor free, nor is there male and female, for you are all one in Christ Jesus."

The Bible clearly teaches that prostitution and immorality are evils in society and have terrible consequences.

Proverbs 5:3-4 "For the lips of the adulterous woman drip honey, and her speech is smoother than oil; but in the end she is bitter as gall, sharp as a double-edged sword."

Matthew 15:18-19 "But the things that come out of a person's mouth come from the heart, and these defile them. For out of the heart come evil thoughts—murder, adultery, sexual immorality, theft, false testimony, slander."

I Corinthians 6:18-19 "Flee from sexual immorality. All other sins a person commits are outside the body, but whoever sins sexually, sins against their own body. Do you not know that your bodies are temples of the Holy Spirit, who is in you, whom you have received from God?"

Galatians 5:19-21 "When you follow the desires of your sinful nature, the results are very clear: sexual immorality, impurity, lustful pleasures… anyone living that sort of life will not inherit the Kingdom of God."

I Thessalonians 4:3 "It is God's will that you should be sanctified: that you should avoid sexual immorality."

Revelation 21:8 "But the cowardly, the unbelieving, the vile, the murderers, the sexually immoral, those who practice magic arts, the idolaters and all liars—they will be consigned to the fiery lake of burning sulfur. This is the second death."

The persons forced into prostitution and immoralities are not the guilty ones nor does God condemn them. Matthew 18:6 gives a warning to every trafficker, pimp and madam. "If you cause one of these little ones who trusts in me to fall into sin, it would be better for you to have a large millstone tied around your neck and be drowned in the depths of the sea."

In one prostitute's own words: *"Prostitution is terrible. The ramifications of the sex industry are so great. No human being should have to be subjected to working in the sex industry. Until you've been there, and you've experienced the demoralization and dehumanization, there's no way that you could condone it."*

It is impossible for a prostituted person to maintain wholeness in the process. Before another entire generation is prostituted, enlist in the fight against Sex Slavery. Prostituted girls are *broken flowers* that need to be restored, to be able to bloom again as beautiful vibrant flowers. [22]

3 Supply and Demand

If people who have morally lost their way continue to demand unlawful sex, then the pimps, madams, and sex traffickers will keep up the supply.

I want to tell you a story about a broken flower I met at the Dream Home. **Jasmine** was sexually abused by her father, stepfathers and uncles, and emotionally abused by her mother.

Her first boyfriend, Victor the Man, fathered her first child and then "turned her out." This began many years of being prostituted along with her sisters and mother. You might say that prostitution became the family business. Over time, Jasmine had more children, *not always knowing who the fathers were*; thus, they were known as trick babies.

Another pimp came into her life that was the violent type, named D.J. Brown. On one occasion he made her get down on her knees, and fired a gun several times over her head and threatened to kill her if she left him. If you think branding slaves ended with the antebellum era, you are mistaken. D.J. branded Jasmine with a hot iron. She once was beaten, raped, and left for dead after being taken outside the city and left on the side of the road by nonpaying clients.

Her next pimp daddy, Mr. Sunshine, was handsome, and Jasmine really fell for him.

He was known as a "Romeo" pimp, playing the role of a lover, which is something these girls desperately need.

He sired over a dozen children among his sex slaves.

Pimps commonly have violent, unprotected sex *with their sex slaves* to maintain dominance and because a pregnant prostitute is a "special product" to some clients. Undoubtedly, this does result in "keeping power," but the pimps rarely remain financially responsible for their offspring. Their children often end up in foster care, orphanages, with a relative, trafficked or sold. It is part of the sad bitter cycle of Sex Slavery.

Many days Jasmine would function on just four to five hours of sleep and minimal food. Her $1,000 daily quota had to be met before she could return home. Client appointments ran anywhere from ten minutes to overnight. Jasmine would be advertised on websites for "$80 an hour." Often Mr. Sunshine would monitor her appointments by cell phone for the entire duration to maintain control, be sure of her safety, and ensure that payment would be made.

Oftentimes, Jasmine was trafficked from place to place to keep revenue flowing. When hungry, she had to sneak off for a quick sandwich or wait until the end of the day to eat something. Many girls in the stable (there are usually five to ten) developed eating disorders, since bulimia was encouraged, and the pimp dispensed laxatives.

Mr. Sunshine lost some shine the day Jasmine ran for her freedom. I am happy to report that as of this writing she is "out of the life" and reunited with her children. Today this broken flower is seeking a new life.

Twenty-five years ago who would have ever dreamed that there would be a system such as the Internet, right at your fingertips, where if you can imagine something, you can word search it, find it, click on it, and have it appear right before your eyes?

These graphic Internet files are available (digitized photographs and artwork - some containing sound and video) to be downloaded and participated in through interactive forums, posts, chat rooms, and by sharing live visuals with others.

Our world of high-speed cyber technology is inundating men, women, boys, and girls with the newest and most subtle addiction in history. Some have lost their jobs, their integrity, and even their families over this addiction.

Yes, almost everyone on the planet has realized that the Internet is an incredible tool for good but equally so, it has become an incredible tool for evil by those who are greedy and heartless. These vipers use it to victimize and entrap and lead astray innocent people, who find themselves taken captive by the sex industry.

The statistics are truly staggering. According to compiled numbers from respected news and research organizations, every second $3,075 is spent on pornography. Every second, 28,258 Internet users are viewing pornography. In that same second 372 Internet users are typing adult search terms into search engines.

The following is a chart of the Top Word Search Requests for Google: [1]

sex	338,000,000
porn	277,000,000
porno	226,000,000
XXX	83,100,000
nude	68,000,000
free porn	55,600,000
porn hub	55,600,000
XNXX	45,500,000
free sex	24,900,000
porno tube	20,400,000
Playboy	20,400,000
sex videos	16,600,000

All of these search words are in the millions. As viewers become increasingly desensitized to sex images, their appetite for more sordid images grows.

77

Playboy is a perfect example of this.

Hugh Hefner founded *Playboy* in 1953. By the 1960s and into the 1970s *Playboy* expanded around the globe. In 1971 circulation of the magazine hit 7.2 million. However, like most print publications *Playboy* is now struggling to survive against rivals such as *Hustler, Penthouse* and the Internet. By October 2009 its circulation was down to 2.6 million, and by July 2010 *Playboy* could only claim a circulation of 1.5 million. Today, the company derives only one-third of its revenue from *Playboy* magazine with the other two-thirds coming from adult content in electronic form, such as television, Internet and DVDs.[2]

Internet pornography statistics disclose that there are about 4.2 million pornographic websites, with 420 million page hits daily. On any given day emails containing pornography average 2.5 billion. Internet pornographic sales are 4.9 billion dollars annually.[3] It is a market-based economy that exists on principles of *supply and demand*. The worldwide demand is absolutely enormous. It is available to anyone who chooses to collect it, download it, and use it for his or her own sexual gratification.

In the United States, child pornography alone generates an estimated 3 billion dollars annually. Every thirty-nine minutes a new pornographic video is being created in America. Over 100 million are being sold or rented annually. The United States is by far the *top producer* of pornographic web pages worldwide with 244,661,900 pages or eighty-nine percent. *It's big business.* [4]

The pornography industry has larger revenues than Microsoft, Google, Amazon, eBay, Yahoo, Apple, and Netflix combined. [5]

As far as addiction goes, Cybersex is the crack cocaine of the Internet.

Internet infidelity has become the new cause of marriage break-ups. In a survey conducted by the American Academy of Matrimonial Lawyers, 63% of attorneys said that online affairs were the leading cause of divorce cases. [6]

In a Homeland Security article title: "Interpol

Official Discusses Human Trafficking and Internet Pornography," by Eugen Tomiuc, Hamish McCulloch, the assistant director of Interpol (International Criminal Police Organization) and the head of the agency's human trafficking division, discusses the problems of both Human Trafficking and child pornography on the Internet. His comments were made at a three-day conference in Noordwijk, the Netherlands, held to consider the policing of human trafficking, as well as issues of international security, illegal immigration, and cybercrime. They found in their study that one company in the United States operated for five months selling access to child pornography sites at $29.95 each and grossed $5.5 million. [7]

We now have Sexaholics Anonymous, Sexual Compulsives Anonymous, Sex Addicts Anonymous, and Sexual Recovery Anonymous. These groups are helping people with hyper sexuality.

Yes, cybersex is both a male (71%) and female (29%) issue. [8] Men, understand your role in God's plan. We are to guard, protect and care for our families. God is our Father, and these girls are His daughters and our sisters. We are to role model a healthy, safe man for our sons. This role is so vital not only for the safety of our children but for those in the community as well. Continue to be mindful that every young girl trapped in Sex Slavery is someone's daughter.

It is estimated that 75% of the girls on these websites, regardless of what they are wearing or not wearing are being sold daily as sex slaves.

Whenever you click on a pornography site, whether paid or free, whether you went looking for it or it came looking for you, THAT CLICK CREATES DEMAND! That demand means the petals of a precious flower are crushed before it could bloom.

Pornography will rob you of God's design for intimacy in your marriage. In most cases, your spouse is never going to look like the girl you find online, potentially, making you a dissatisfied husband. Matthew 5:27-28 says, "You have heard that it was said, 'You shall not commit adultery.' But I tell you that anyone who looks at a woman lustfully has already committed adultery with her in his heart."

It is my goal to slow this demand by helping men understand that these victims are forced, beaten, and threatened to perform these sex acts.

I want you to read the following definition again so it will permeate your mind and hopefully compel you to become part of the army that is fighting against Sex Slavery.

According to Polaris Project, a forerunner in fighting human trafficking in the United States; after drug trafficking, human trafficking is the second most prolific criminal industry in the world, producing 32 billion dollars annually which is six times more than Google, Nike, and Starbucks combined.[9]

On February 3, 2008, at the Super Bowl XLII, in Phoenix, Arizona, three teenage girls were trafficked by a Miami, Florida pimp. He advertised these girls on Craigslist, and as it was being monitored by local law enforcement, he was busted, and the girls were set free. Hold that thought for a minute… In 1893, the Chicago's World's Fair had 27.5 million in attendance when the entire nation's population stood at 65 million. The Fair introduced Americans to the Pledge of Allegiance, Juicy Fruit gum and the Ferris wheel, *and to teenage girls being trafficked for sex from New York, St. Louis, and other cities!* [10]

What do these two events that are separated by 115 years have in common? A demand and supply for sex. As you read this book, ask yourselves, "Am I contributing to the problem?"

A prostituted street worker's average daily intake is $1,000, and most pimps have six working girls. [11] They may serve as many as 10-20 clients a day, every day. [12]

What type of emotional pain do you think these victims go through? Can you feel their anguish at all? Will you consider doing something that I do? Send up a prayer now and then for victims who want to run for their freedom. It could mean life or death for them. Psalm 6:9 says, "The LORD has heard my cry for mercy; the LORD accepts my prayer."

As stated, men are primarily, but not solely the perpetrators; they create the demand and the emotional pain and abuse. You may say, "What I do on my computer, my phone, the movies and DVD's I watch on my TV, or the magazines I buy, doesn't hurt anyone. I am not buying sex on the street or visiting a strip club or going to a massage parlor." It's all the same, men - as long as you create demand there will need to be a supply!

Immigration and Customs Enforcement (I.C.E.) agents at the Cyber Crimes Center in Fairfax, Virginia, are finding that when it comes to sex, what was once considered abnormal is now the norm. They are trafficking a clear spike in the demand for harder-core pornography on the Internet. "We have become desensitized by the soft stuff: now we need a harder and harder hit," says I.C.E. Special Agent Perry Woo. Cyber networks through which you can download and trade images and videos have become the Mexican border of virtual sexual exploitation. With the use of cyber networks, sex slaves can be auctioned to individuals for as much as $300,000. [13]

This demand should be the motivation for every good man to become a guardian and protector of all women.

If couples engage in sexual activity that requires voices, pictures, or videos to "spice up" their marriage, either directly or indirectly they increase the demand for Sex Slavery. The book of Hebrews says, "Marriage should be honored by all, and the marriage bed kept pure, for God will judge the adulterer and all the sexually immoral."

For those who are married, realize to live FREE of all pornography in your marriage is to live a FULL relationship. For those who are waiting to get married, realize to live FREE of all pornography in your singleness is to live FULL in your future marriage relationship. Aspire to be a godly person. Practice self-discipline, loyalty and honor. Free yourself from sexual addiction, and live a full life! Titus 2:11-13 says, "For the grace of God has appeared that offers salvation to all people. It teaches us to say 'No' to ungodliness and worldly passions, and to live self-controlled, upright and godly lives in this present age, while we wait for the blessed hope—the appearing of the glory of our great God and Savior, Jesus Christ". Salvation makes one connected to the Lord and gives you the power to say "NO!'

To win the battle of supply and demand we have to raise moral standards at every opportunity and in every venue.

If you need further help, go to the runforfreedom.net resource page and click on "Effects of Cyber Sex" and use filters on your computers such as "CyberSitter," "HomeGuard," or "Safe Eyes."

Together, let's end the demand for more supply!

4 It's All About the Money

Growing up in the 70s I was inundated with Pink Floyd's music. Their 1973 Album, "The Dark Side of the Moon," which contains the song, "Money," sold over 34 million copies. I can still hear the tune in my head. Most people thought it was written in a positive light but to the contrary. One of the verses says, "Money, so they say is the root of all evil today." The message is more about the bad things money can do. "Grab that cash with both hands and make a stash." Those who are exploiting young girls in the sex industry today are doing just that, and most of the "stash" has to be laundered to make it clean.

When it comes to Sex Slavery in America, many people have limited knowledge. To help you become more aware, allow me to use the analogy of being invited as a guest to someone's home. You accept the invitation and arrive on time. Once at the front door you ring the doorbell. The door is opened and greetings are exchanged. You then take your first step into the entryway, and your host leads you into the kitchen where there is an aroma of freshly brewed coffee. Soon you are led into the living room where recently baked apple turnovers are waiting on the center table next to the bright Orange gerbera daisies. You take your seat on the couch and engage in warm and wholesome conversation. You depart after a while, expressing your gratitude for a nice visit. However, you never entered the private, more remote areas of the home, such as the bedrooms, the closets, the basement, or the attic. Rightly so; these are the personal areas and sometimes the places where secrets are kept.

In a moment I will take you to those private areas beyond the kitchen and living room where the conversation is not so pleasant, and there are no sweet aromas but rather a stench to your nostrils that you won't forget. These closed doors have to be opened for you to be enlightened. Exposing these areas will

bring us deeper into the driving force of Sex Slavery...
money.

Does it surprise you to know
that Sex Slavery is not motivated
primarily by lust and sex but
rather by greed?

According to MSNBC, a pimp with three sex slaves
in the Washington, D.C. area can make as much as
$500,000 a year. An average brothel in America can
earn as much as $250,000 a month. [1]

Almost all of this money is "under the table" so
the Internal Revenue Service can't tax it. Such "dirty
money" is only useful after it has been cleaned. Forensic
accountants are experts trained to see beyond the
numbers recorded in the ledgers. In their fight against
Sex Slavery and laundered money they have learned
at least three things:

1. Members of international rings who are
greedy and deceitful recruit young girls from
other countries and entice them with promises
of jobs and a prosperous future.

2. Once the girls are convinced, they help them obtain their travel documents to America. The incurred debt is required but impossible to be paid back. As they are sold daily as sex slaves and the money given to their captors, their debt bondage becomes a never-ending nightmare.

3. Some financial institutions and real estate establishments receive deposits of large amounts of cash from these horrendous crimes.

As said before, once girls are lured in and become property of their captors they are threatened, beaten, and raped in order to maintain control over them so the money flow continues.

This dirty money is made at venues such as massage parlors, spas, escort services, strip clubs, private homes, online sex sites, the streets, and in brothels.

This "need for greed" and love of money causes the human heart to become calloused and grow cold. Husbands, fathers, brothers, and boyfriends have coerced their own wives, daughters, sisters and girlfriends to earn money for them as sex slaves. Shockingly, even mothers have sold their daughters at very young ages and in their very own homes.

Behind one closed bedroom door in a local American neighborhood. **Rose,** an American teenager from a middle-upper class family who was held in bondage for two years as a sex slave. Her captors were two high school classmates. What follows is a horrible and painful bedroom scene that took place behind closed doors, in a room where Rose was met by several men.

One of the men pulled out several pieces of rope. Rose had a bad feeling about this and nervously shivered. Another guy grabbed her leg and tied it to the corner of the bed. She lay there spread eagle, humiliated at being rudely exposed. Tears of shame flooded her eyes. One by one, the men in the room abused her. Rose screamed in agony and pleaded with the men to stop. From the pain, fear, and lack of air, she hyperventilated. The agony seemed to last for hours. Lack of circulation had caused her legs to go numb, while the rest of her body burned with pain. She went into shock from the abuse. Mercifully, she lost consciousness.[2]

You may ask, "How can this be?" The unfortunate simple answer is…it's all about the money.

For these "wannabe" high school gangsters it was always about the money, and by their evil hands this precious flower was broken.

I had the privilege of meeting Rose at a conference in Orlando, Florida and today she is raising awareness and soon to open a home in Ohio for victims.

An estimated two million women and children are sold into Sex Slavery around the world every year. [3] Money laundering is an important part of the process.

Money Laundering includes any act or attempt to disguise the source of money or assets derived from criminal activity that produces large profits: illegal arms, insider trading, computer fraud, smuggling, illegal immigration, bribery, drug trafficking, embezzlement, and Sex Slavery. [4]

According to the U.S. Department of State,

international trafficking in women and children, smuggling of migrants and contraband, money laundering, cybercrime, theft of intellectual property rights, vehicle theft, public corruption, environmental crimes, and trafficking in small arms cost U.S. taxpayers and businesses billions of dollars each year. [5]

Forbes Magazine published an article entitled, "Money Laundering, Gun-running, Sex Slavery," which questioned if Cyprus is becoming a tax haven, considering the link between violence and money. According to the article, Cyprus has a thriving sex trade that draws women from former Soviet states. An immigration chief was reportedly jailed for twenty months after being found guilty of accepting bribes to issue work permits for foreign women to work in cabarets. According to the author, some 2,000 women per year arrive in Cyprus to work in these clubs, often under compulsion, helping to generate $70 million per year in prostitution revenue and fees for pimps who work in the women's home countries and broker the traffic. [6]

There are worldwide initiatives along with local initiatives and assistance programs in place to protect the United States from such threats, but all countries are exposed to these crimes. The challenge is to target the criminals who exploit desperate people and to protect and assist victims of trafficking, as well as smuggled migrant workers, many of whom endure unimaginable hardships in their bid for a better life.[7]

Atlanta, Georgia has become the new sex tourist hot spot for Americans.

A sex buyer no longer needs to fly to Thailand or the Philippines; customers can place their order online in the morning, fly to Atlanta to do their sex thing, and be back home with their wife and kids for dinner like nothing never happened. [8]

Pornography revenue in America supersedes all professional football, baseball, and basketball franchises in the United States combined. [9]

My opening analogy suggested the need to go further, beyond the kitchen to expose the awful cruelties of the sex industry.

The power of greed is so strong that such an

evil as "snuff" films exists. A snuff film depicts the actual murder of a person or people, without the aid of special effects, for the express purpose of distribution and entertainment for financial profit. [10]

One terrible story told to me was of a young virgin girl who was gang raped so she would intentionally hyperventilate and pass out in the act, or die from exhaustion. These films are prepared in a few hours; placed on a website, and in just one month can gross a million dollars.

I realize you might ask in shock and wonder, "How can someone commit such a horrifying act?" It's all about the money! God help us!

The 2007 movie *Trade* is based on a *New York Times* article entitled, "The Girls Next Door," written by Peter Landesman, a freelance journalist who followed trafficked girls from the Mexican border all the way to New Jersey. The border patrol officers were granted sexual favors to look the other way, letting traffickers and their prey into America. The new recruits' clothing was exchanged for more enticing attire, and their photographs were taken so the online bidding could begin.

On the way to New Jersey, the girls realized the promised better job was not what was awaiting them, but rather something terrible. After being beaten and abused, one of these *broken flowers* tragically committed suicide. After several days, the remaining girls arrived in a New Jersey neighborhood at a typical "house next door." The buyers also arrived to "test" the merchandise, make payment, and take their newly acquired property home. [11]

The 2008 movie *Taken* (a must see) woke up half the world to this nightmare. It offers an excellent portrayal of the amount of money offered at a typical auction, based on a real raid that took place in Miami, Florida. Realistically, few victims have a father with the special tactical skills such as actor Liam Neeson portrayed as he took out the Albanian Mafia single-handedly. Most would not rebound back to everyday life as quickly as his daughter did at the end. In fact, it is doubtful one would ever make it home at all.

On an equally dark side, the money making does not stop with just selling victims for sex. As sex slaves lose their working value, in some cases their organs are made available for sale on the black market.

In July 2009, United States agents arrested 44 elected officials and Jewish rabbis in a huge anti-corruption sweep across New Jersey. Charges of extortion, bribery, money laundering, and human organ trafficking were shocking, even for a state known for corruption and organized crime. This was literally blood money. [12]

In May 2010, *Run for Freedom* discovered firsthand when two Slovakian women trafficked from Chicago were rescued. Immigration Custom Enforcement (I.C.E.) of Orlando, Florida completed their investigation, and it turned out that they were not trafficked to Florida for the sex industry but for their kidneys. I learned a kidney could sell for as much as $30,000 on the black market.

Money laundering is the act of taking a series of steps to make illegal money appear legitimate.

Money Laundering has often been applied to the profits of drug trafficking, but as Sex Slavery grows in scope and profitability, the term is associated with this business, as well.

To launder their money, traffickers use bank transfers, accounting tricks, bribes to public officials, and other means. They also use middlemen or even victims to move money around so they are able to keep their distance and avoid being caught.

Funds are often wire transferred to several foreign bank accounts in various countries under fictitious names. Investments are made in legal cash based businesses (bars, restaurants, nail salons). Often these businesses play a dual role. Dirty money buys the business, and victims are forced to work in them. Businesses are used as fronts with little to no actual business being conducted. The good news is that all laundering still leaves an electronic paper trail behind for law enforcement to follow.

The Scottish Crime and Drug Enforcement Agency reports that their forensic accountants have conducted a number of money laundering investigations. They have utilized complex audit trails as supporting evidence in prosecuting major criminals for money laundering. Forensic accountants can make a difference by helping law enforcement and investigators bring criminals to justice. [13]

The infamous mob boss Al Capone was finally jailed on tax evasion charges, not for the multiple homicides, conspiracies, and other serious crimes that he was wanted for at the time. Today, law enforcement agents are taking a tip from their forefathers who caught Capone by looking at creative ways to arrest cunning sex traffickers. If law enforcement arrested Al Capone for not paying his income taxes, then they are certainly able to find traffickers who haven't thoroughly washed their cash.

It would be nice if there were a law that allowed confiscated dirty money to be given to causes that fight against the very crime that the money came from.

Now that you have gone beyond the living room where you were sipping on your coffee and eating your apple turnover, enjoying the beauty of the Orange gerbera daisies and talking about trouble-free things, what if one of these victims was your daughter, sister, or friend? How would you respond? These victims are someone's daughter, sister, and friend! I ask again, how will you respond?

5 The Cause for Justice

What do you think of when you see a nine-year-old little blond-haired, blue-eyed American girl? Words that come to my mind are happy, innocent, cute, sweet, princess, doll, playful, pure, gullible, blameless, amiable, carefree, virtuous, angelic, honest, charming, adorable, good, naive, trusting, unblemished, lovable, and free. I surprised myself with almost two-dozen words, and I think most people would agree with me. You may even have some of your own to add, and by all means, please do.

Unfortunately, when some people in this world think of a nine-year-old little blond-haired, blue-eyed American girl, although they may think these same things, they also think of exploiting her because of their twisted sexual interest in prepubescent children.

I want to tell you a story about a little blond-haired American girl who came to the Dream Home. A neighborhood man in his forties deflowered **Violet** at the age of nine. He took advantage of her naivety and groomed her as his personal sex slave for his own sexual gratification. He made videos of her and other neighborhood children to keep for his private use. This abuse went on for several years. In return, she received payment in the form of fast food, cigarettes, and small gifts.

When she was fifteen-years-old another older local man came along. He joined in on taking advantage of her. He too justified it by lowering or waiving rent and buying groceries. These men robbed Violet of her freedom, innocence, and youth. By her late teens she was promiscuous, on medication, in and out of juvenile homes, plagued with nightmares and had attempted suicide more than once. She never developed like the other girls her age and became emotionally stuck in her pain, grief, and anger. Violet is a broken flower in need of restoration. My heart breaks over the injustice done to this blond-haired American girl. The injustice of Sex Slavery even reaches the girl next door.

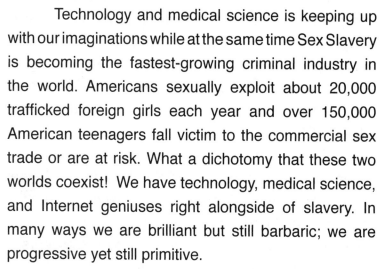

Technology and medical science is keeping up with our imaginations while at the same time Sex Slavery is becoming the fastest-growing criminal industry in the world. Americans sexually exploit about 20,000 trafficked foreign girls each year and over 150,000 American teenagers fall victim to the commercial sex trade or are at risk. What a dichotomy that these two worlds coexist! We have technology, medical science, and Internet geniuses right alongside of slavery. In many ways we are brilliant but still barbaric; we are progressive yet still primitive.

You might think that it is happening in the big cities, and you're right. But if you think it only exists in the big cities then you are sadly mistaken. It is happening in small rural communities, in trailer parks, on construction sites, and in private homes in suburban neighborhoods.

105

> In the U.S., California is first, - New York is the second, - and Florida is the third - most trafficked state.[1]

As I mentioned before, sex slaves are forced into prostitution and often sold 10 to 20 times daily.[2] They have NO FREEDOM, NO RIGHTS; they are held against their will; they have been wronged, grieved, deeply wounded, and they live in fear. There is a word that clearly describes this cruelty, and that is INJUSTICE!

Sex Slavery has become the new Global Slave Trade. It involves more people than the 400-year Trans-Atlantic Slave Trade that took place between the fourteenth and nineteenth centuries.[3] Sex Slavery has been hidden beneath the surface for over 150 years.

What about injustice? Injustice applies to any act that involves unfairness to another or violation of another's freedom.

Isaiah 58:6 has something very profound to say, "Is not this the kind of fasting I have chosen: to loose the chains of injustice and untie the cords of the yoke, to set the oppressed free and break every yoke?"

According to this verse, God is calling us to loose chains of injustice and set the oppressed free. Justice demands action. We cannot sit idly by and do nothing.

A sex slave is told where to go, what to say, what to do. SHE HAS NO FREEDOM! Every human being has a right to be free, and we have a responsibility to each other.

Who are these girls sold into slavery? These victims are children of God and therefore our very own family.

Picture this, a young lady is wined and dined by her bogus Prince Charming. He pretends to be a gentleman in every aspect. He leads her on and proposes to marry her. Once he wins her confidence she is asked to travel with him to meet his family. The catch is, they live in another country and travel documents are required.

Just imagine her emotions as they are traveling, somewhat anxious, a little nervous but very excited. In just a short time the photos that she has seen and the stories she has heard of his family will be a reality. As they approach the house and she goes through the door with anticipation and delight, something seems wrong to her. All of a sudden, she is grabbed by a strange man and pulled away. She may be beaten and raped immediately. At the same time, she sees her prince being handed a roll of money. He goes back out the door, leaving her bewildered, alone and afraid. She screams out his name to no avail. She is then immediately shamed and mistreated as the new property of an evil, greedy captor. Another broken flower. Now that is an injustice!

As was mentioned previously, pimps often brand their prostitutes with tattoos as a mark of "ownership", this is a part of their seasoning. A prominent pimp who is a Boston Celtics fan brands a green clover on the left ankle of his girls to show that they are his property. That is an injustice! [4]

Debt bondage is a common tool used in Sex Slavery. Innocent people are tricked, trapped, transported, and/or enticed into a "land of opportunity." Once involved, there is usually no way out. Upon enlistment they are told that the expenses for travel, clothing and housing are considered as a "loan" that they must pay back. They work seven days a week and never seem to be able to work off the original loan.

Various forms of threats and force are used to ensure control. In many cases the victims are kept under surveillance, sometimes under lock and key.

Debt bondage exists when the value of services

rendered are not reasonably assessed nor applied towards the liquidation of the debt, or the length and nature of those services are not respectively limited and defined. Because additional debt for clothes, food, housing, and medical bills continues to accrue, it is a never-ending debt. That is an injustice! [5]

Arrests take place across America; unfortunately, they are prostitutes who are forced and sex slaves rather than the slick pimps and traffickers. When **Lily,** was left alone for a few minutes in a hotel room in Orlando, Florida, she sneaked a phone call to her mother. She had only a one-hour window to escape before she would be trafficked to Jacksonville, Florida and then on to New Orleans, Louisiana. Her mother called me and explained her situation, and I called a local detective who works with sex trafficking cases. He contacted Lily at the hotel and found out that she had four outstanding warrants for her arrest. He would be obligated to expedite her to South Carolina to answer for the first warrant and subsequently the others as well. When she heard this she changed her mind and fell victim once again to the horrible life of Sex Slavery; another broken flower feeling like she has no way out. That's an injustice!

A West Coast Florida fire chief is on trial for raping and molesting a young neighborhood girl for several years. He used pornographic movies to "groom" her and videotaped her by hiding the camera during the sexual abuse. That is not uncommon in cases of child sexual abuse, says David Finkelhor director of The Crimes Against Children Research Center at the University of New Hampshire. "These cases often start out with grooming the kid to accept it for the attention, or making a game out of it, or normalizing it," he said. "But then, when the kid begins to get older and realizes that this is really not cool, offenders begin to bargain with them over stuff they want. Victims of long-term sexual abuse sometimes engage in this type of bartering and keep the abuse to themselves because they've been indoctrinated to believe it is normal behavior." These *broken flowers* will need long term emotional and spiritual help. That is an injustice! [6]

On August 20, 2010, in Orange County, Florida, the trial of 39-year-old man was held before a county judge for the kidnapping of a 15-year-old girl who was walking home from school. She was beaten, raped and forced with a weapon to live as a sex slave. He had trafficked her to Lake County, Florida where the teenager was held captive in a garage and brought to a mobile home park in Minneola, Florida. She had sex with sixty men over twenty-one days while the kidnapper received the money. Luckily, the girl's mother was tipped off to her daughter's whereabouts and authorities rescued her. He pleaded guilty to the crimes and "got his day in court" one would think. However, the judge said, "Mr. _____, your sentence is one year of which you already served waiting trial. I am giving you two years probation." Another flower broken. That is an injustice!

Mr. _____ had one request: that he could serve out his sentence in the state of Georgia. His request was granted by the state of Florida. After the sentencing, while he was being finger printed, a WFTV reporter asked him "How could you have done this to a 15-year-old girl?" His response was vulgar and arrogant. [7]

Martin Luther, the reformer, once said, "Injustice anywhere threatens justice everywhere."

Those who are treated unjustly can't fight for themselves; they need need our help to gain freedom! Again, Isaiah the prophet said, "Is not this the kind of fasting I have chosen: to loose the chains of injustice and untie the cords of the yoke, to set the oppressed free and break every yoke?"

On the occasion of the 200th anniversary of the eradication of the slave trade in Great Britain, the film *Amazing Grace* was released, depicting the life of abolitionist William Wilberforce, who championed the cause even when supporters were few. Despite fierce opposition from members of Parliament who were connected with plantation owners, Wilberforce persevered. William Pitt and John Newton, a former slave-ship captain turned evangelical preacher, aided him in his quest. William Wilberforce could not do it alone.

The wall of injustice is too massive, too solid, and too difficult for any one person or organization to take it down. But together we can take this wall down.

On December 23, 2008 President George W. Bush signed a bill into law that enhanced measures to combat human trafficking. The bill, which was passed by voice vote in the House and unanimous consent in the Senate, authorized appropriations for 2008 through 2011 for the Trafficking Victims Protection Act of 2008. It is called the William Wilberforce Trafficking Victims Protection Reauthorization Act of 2008. [8]

Jesus came; lived, and died so all people could be free, free of sin, free of oppression, and free from the chains of injustice.

Let's stop the injustice of Sex Slavery in America!

6 Run for Freedom Story

Wow! It is so cool to travel back and reflect on the Run for Freedom story. There have been so many awesome people I have met, what kindness, compassion, love and generosity! Oftentimes I have been overwhelmed with the extravagant goodness of these individuals who have become an integral part of this journey. Numerous miracles create an ongoing excitement in the hearts of those who have joined the Run for Freedom army. Later on, I will tell you about this army and how none of this story would be possible without the obvious fingerprints of the Divine. He is seen throughout and that really makes this His story!

Why would God, who rules the universe and holds everything in check, want to involve Himself in our story? With so much going on in the world, why would one sex slave girl, one broken flower, concern Him?

One night as I positioned myself very near to the heart of God, close enough to hear His heartbeat, it was then that I realized Sex Slavery breaks the heart of God.

As a young man, I always found myself defending the underdog, the outcast, and the one nobody seemed to care about. It just seemed to be in my DNA. By my early twenties, I came to Christ and found myself walking away from all my worldly ambitions for wealth and success (that is, success that is measured by material possessions) to make a difference in people's lives.

Even though most of my peers would have changed positions with me in a heartbeat, I deeply felt that people mattered more than money or things. So I spent the prime years of my life helping broken, discarded, and hurting people. In the process, I have traveled on every continent experiencing food poisoning, exhaustion at times, sleep deprivation, and hunger. I have bathed in dirty rivers, and once I was even taken at gun point. Understand, I take no personal honor in this; it was due to a desire that was formed in me when I came to Christ. I believe these years were the foundation for me to now stand securely in the fight to make a difference against Sex Slavery in America, and to help free its victims.

Around fifteen years ago I conceived the idea of Dream Again Ministries and made business cards and letterhead with the slogan "Bringing Hope to the Brokenhearted." Later, Dream Again Ministries secured a 501(c)(3) designation to operate as a non-profit. A subsidiary, Run for Freedom, was established when we became concerned about the number of Americans lacking knowledge about the atrocity of Sex Slavery.

On October 24, 2005 a movie was released on the Lifetime Channel entitled *Human Trafficking*.

The main actors are Mira Sorvino and Donald Sutherland. In 2006, when it re-aired, I watched it.

Let me back up a bit. For years my three children

would always say, "Dad why are you watching the girl channel?" This channel is also known as the man haters channel because many of the story lines are about men doing terrible things to women. My answer was, "I want to know what the women feel when men mistreat them and have a better understanding of what makes men treat these women as if they have no value."

Human Trafficking depicts how young girls vanish from their everyday lives, forced by violence into a hellish existence of brutality and prostitution. It certainly educates the naive audiences who are under the impression that Sex Slavery does not exist. Director Christian Duguay's Golden Globe nomination proves he did a superb job in portraying the subject and he certainly depicted how lucrative this multi-billion-dollar industry is. The script clearly intended to educate the audience with Sex Slavery facts and leave a lasting impression about its horrors.

There are several different kinds of Sex Slavery depicted. One depiction tells of a 12-year-old American girl who is kidnapped while on vacation overseas. During her mother's tireless efforts to find her, she learns about the world of the international sex trade.

I.C.E. officers are portrayed as determined to fight back and stop criminals from committing these horrendous crimes.

As I watched, I was certainly disturbed by what I saw and heard, but I am troubled by a lot of things.

In February of 2008 I was home alone, and saw *Human Trafficking* was coming on TV again. I grabbed a pen and a yellow lined pad to take notes. As a public speaker, I am always looking for accurate facts and good story lines; I knew this movie had both. I sat in my recliner, and little did I know I would never be the same.

It seemed like an eternity before the three-hour movie ended. At one point I looked down at my notepaper and noticed the ink was bleeding from my fallen tears. I got so choked up at times I found myself gasping for air. My heart slowly broke in pieces for the young innocent female victims who were held captive by evil hands. The sexual acts they were forced to do made me want to vomit. I was so totally engaged by the end of the movie I was sobbing uncontrollably. Unlike my first viewing of the movie, this time I knew Divinity was at work in me and I sensed Him say,

119

"I want you to do something about this. I want you to make a difference".

Several things transpired that night, as my heart was broken before the Lord. I realized to accomplish this huge assignment I needed to know the specifics of the mission. I knew I would have to resign my position and begin to live "by faith" financially, something I hadn't needed to be concerned about for over thirty years.

I would have to find a home for rescued victims (which was a lot easier said than done) and build an informative and preventive website that would actually help people avoid the snare of Sex Slavery. Last but not at all least, I definitely needed a small army of people to assist me.

Within months, my wife Mary Ann and I launched "Run For Freedom" to raise awareness and to establish Dream Homes in America for female victims (both domestic and international) of Sex Slavery.

The first idea among many was to hold 5K's where walkers and runners would wear Orange to represent FREEDOM for those enslaved by Sex Slavery.

Thus the name "Run for Freedom", referring to the feeling so many associate with running; that feeling of freedom from all the stuff that has a way of clinging to you and bringing you down. Everyone has the right to be free… free from control, from abuse, from stress, and from pain, free to be who God created you to be and to live life to the fullest.

Sadly, every day young girls are bought and sold; others have interfered with their sovereignty, using coercion and aggression to subject them to Sex Slavery. It is our desire to see these victims *run for freedom* from their enslavement. Now that the first Dream Home has opened in Central Florida, and the plan is to open others to follow, victims have a refuge where they can run to their freedom!

The first miracle was acquiring the Dream Home property, which I will expound on in Chapter 8. The following describes just a portion of the army of people, businesses, organizations, and churches that made the Dream Home a reality. The list is too extensive to elaborate on each story.

When we took ownership of the Dream Home, one of the first things that had to be done was cut the grass. Mary Ann decided to run her fingers through the *Yellow Pages* and make a few cold calls to local bushwhackers. One man said yes, came, and tackled the multiple acres free of charge.

When the workload felt overwhelming and the house needed power washing I began to pray and an hour later a man called and said, "I will take care of it." Wow! The army was on the way! He and a retired couple painted every room in the Dream Home, with most of the paint donated or purchased at a reduced price.

One local church from Orlando, Florida decided to put hands and feet to their faith and brought the whole church body to the Dream Home one Sunday morning. They removed large tree branches to make room for the horses, mowed several acres, and pruned fruit trees and shrubs. They left behind a brand new gas grill, a riding lawn mower, two picnic tables and a mile high burn pile!

A mission team flew to Florida all the way from Rhode Island to take on the dock project. The dock extends 165 feet out into the lake. It has a 300 square foot covering. They secured the dock and installed lighting, ceiling fans, side ropes, and railings. In this very serene area students and staff are able to meet for counseling, meditation, fishing, and alligator watching. This team also rebuilt the porch stairs, put in flagstone walks, and helped with several other inside projects. They supplied all the funding and travel expense.

Soon afterwards, a Massachusetts mission team arrived and built a prayer gazebo in a lovely tranquil setting, providing another outdoor quiet place for staff and students. They also tackled many small interior projects but the grandest of all was completely renovating the two-car garage into a beautiful chapel/learning center. Before they left we dedicated the entire property to God to transform lives. These two pastors and church teams were awesome!

A week later I was sharing in a local church about how grateful I was for the team and all they accomplished. I mentioned we needed air conditioning and the proprietor of an cooling and heating company came the next day to the Dream Home. He did the entire installation at no charge!

About three hundred feet in front of the Dream Home there was a 30' x 40' foot broken down garage. In just six weeks it was transformed into a three-stall barn for the therapy animals, complete with a bathroom. With the help of three local guys, a carpenter from Rhode Island, an electrician, a father and son plumbing company, and myself, the Freedom Barn was established.

An extraordinary amount of money had to be raised in a short time and by the grace of God many financial miracles took place.

The first was an unsolicited, divine $5,000 check from a wonderful retired couple. This began the necessary income flow. Then I called a friend who oversees a ministry in New England, and he agreed to give another $5,000. A church in Winter Park, Florida also generously gave $5,000. All this assured me that God had called us, and it was evident that He was going to supply all our needs.

A man from Tallahassee, Florida found our website, and was touched by our mission. He called saying he had three daughters and wanted to do something to help, though he was not sure what he could do. A few months later he called saying he had a meeting in the Orlando, Florida area and would like to meet me and see the Dream Home. After our visit, he handed me a check for $5,000. He told me he had sold some stock for a greater profit than he had anticipated. He had planned on giving a lesser amount, but after praying he sensed God told him to give it all.

Our first Sex Trafficking Awareness 5K Fundraiser was held in four locations (Orlando, Florida; Oakland, Florida; Lincoln, Rhode Island; and Fitchburg, Massachusetts) on September 5, 2009. The proceeds were $15,000. We were very encouraged by God's blessing as He continued to show us His faithfulness.

As time progressed, amazingly we began to receive $1,000 checks regularly. The initial $1,000 was from friends who believed in the cause from the very first day they heard about it.

Then I remember the day I met a woman from Lakeland, Florida who came to see the Dream Home.

Even though I never mentioned it to her, I had been praying for funds for fence posts and gates that three local retired ranchers were going to install for us. She sat at the dining room table that day and wrote out a check for $1,000.

A young, single professional woman from Orlando, Florida who was passionate about ending Sex Slavery attended an event we held and gave a check for $1,000. She continues to be involved in helping us further the cause.

I met a wonderful married couple in Maine who sacrificially gave a check for $1,000 that they were saving for a vacation.

There was a dear elderly woman who attended one of our "Dinner and a Movie" events in a wheelchair. She was touched by our mission and also gave a $1,000 check.

One guy who worked on the Dream Home knew we needed some windows replaced and he joined the $1,000 army without hesitation.

While driving to a meeting one day, I shared with a friend about the mobile home we were installing for the caretaker. At the end of the meeting, as we departed, she generously handed me a check for $1,000.

While at a speaking engagement at a church in Massachusetts, as I stood behind our Orange product table, a smiling young woman came by and simply handed me a check for $1,000.

When I shared about Sex Slavery in a Florida pastor's office, tears filled his eyes. He then came to see the Dream Home, returned to his church and sent a check for a $1,000.

After I spoke with a group of pastors in Rhode Island, one of them told his staff about Run for Freedom and that he was sending a $1,000 check. One of them decided to join him and gave a $1,000 check as well.

A young woman who received an unexpected bonus check of $1,000, gave it all to the Dream Home.

Then there was a guy who sent a $1,000 check through his church after hearing my message on "Supply and Demand."

A young, ambitious college student, who is very passionate about making a difference with Run for Freedom, raised $1,000 for a Dream Home project.

One couple, after hearing me speak about Sex Slavery in their Sunday morning church service, was so moved that they went to our website and donated, you guessed it, $1,000.

There is not enough time to tell of the countless stories of others.

Realizing we had almost eight acres of grass, shrubs, a dozen different kinds of fruit trees, therapy animals, a barn, a dock, and the Dream Home...we needed a caretaker. He would not be able to live in the home so we pondered the idea of acquiring a mobile home. One of our neighbors who had been in the business helped us purchase one for half the cost and managed the whole project. I said to him, "I don't know where you came from, but I am sure glad you did."

The proprietor of a local septic company installed the whole system at no charge. Another local man did the plumbing at no charge. The caretaker built the back deck on the mobile home. Each of these were such a huge help. We are so grateful.

On a specific day we all began to fast and pray, and to our amazement that same day we heard a knock at our door. It was someone who had given $1,000 when we first launched Run for Freedom. She explained how the Lord kept bringing my face before her telling her to help me. She said He gave her an amount, but since she was married she had to have confirmation from her husband by him getting the same figure from the Lord himself. Ten days later she returned with her husband while I was out of town. Mary Ann answered the door and invited them in. They handed her an envelope, and as she opened it she was amazed. Once they reached me by phone, Mary Ann said, "Honey, I'm with ____. They came by and brought us a check – guess how much!" I thought, "Oh no! If I guess too low I'll insult them. If I guess too high, I'll embarrass them." So I called on Jesus and I blurted out, "$10,000!" Mary Ann screamed with excitement, "He got the number, too!" We all laughed and praised God.

One day a local group of fifty-five blindfolded church men came by bus to the Dream Home. Why blindfolded? Because it's a secure property. In three and a half hours they transformed the outdoor landscaping by laying wood chips in the pathways, mulching the garden beds, and planting flowers and shrubs. Everything was donated by two local businesses. They pruned, cleaned up, cut branches that were touching the roof, and replaced the back deck of the chapel. They left the property "picture perfect" and totally changed, as will be the lives of the girls who walk on these paths and enjoy the landscaping.

Our new insurance agent whom we had yet to meet in person opened her heart and checkbook by committing to pay our first year insurance premium – over $6,000.

Friends called one day saying they had sold a piece of property and wanted to give us a check for $3,000.

When we met with them the check turned out to be $30,000. We were shocked! That's a lot of money!

They said there were no strings attached and to use it wherever it was needed most. God orchestrated several things for this donation to become ten times the original amount, but it would never have happened without their obedience to Him.

I was in New Hampshire for a weekend and

was greeted by some snow and cold weather. But the warmth of a wonderful pastor and his church blessed us with the largest offering we have ever received.

I met a pastor from Leesburg, Florida at the Dream Home and shared our need to raise funds to pay qualified staff. He was touched and brought it before his leadership – they responded with a $12,000 check.

After doing five services for a church in the South Shore area of Boston, Massachusetts, pastored by a great lady, they took an offering and gave Run for Freedom a check for $3,000. It was the largest gift they had ever given a guest speaker.

A kind pastor in Missouri flew me out to his city, paid all my expenses, gave me the opportunity to speak in two Sunday morning services and took a special offering: $4,500 was the generous response.

One pastor in Massachusetts asked me to share for five minutes about Sex Slavery in America, and then he would take an offering for us. He was delighted to inform me that $3,000 came in.

That reminds me of a church in Florida where I presented the ministry on a Wednesday night. The pastor took two offerings, the first one for his church.

He told the people if they only came prepared to give one offering to save it for Run for Freedom. The check was for $3,000. That church's young adult group also came to the Dream Home with $1,000 to purchase and install our much needed fencing and gates.

Every three months, an Orlando, Florida church goes into the community to make a difference. They came and did all the preparations for our garden and installed fencing and irrigation. They are committed to perform this service on an ongoing basis. Their labor and gift will keep on giving as the girls and staff of the Dream Home will eat and enjoy the future harvests.

Can you imagine furnishing a whole house and somebody else paying for it? Well, several people paid to furnish the Dream Home. The bedroom furniture was paid for by a church; the chapel chairs were bought by a ladies group; the flat screen plasma television and dining room chairs were bought by a Rotary Club; the dining room draperies were designed and purchased by an individual; our kitchen appliances were all donated by friends; our freezers by a gal who has been a volunteer; our chapel/learning center sound system was from a woman's organization; our dining room table from Olive Garden. Wal-Mart, Lowe's, Home Depot, and others all played a role in this wonderful adventure.

A kind woman from the Space Coast of Florida donated a second car she no longer needed.

Another church in New Hampshire took a special offering for Run for Freedom after I spoke in three of their services. This benevolent pastor also told me it was the largest offering they had ever collected for a guest. Then he and his wife personally donated a car for our use when we are in the New England area.

This is the army that the Lord told me He would raise up if I would be obedient and do something about this terrible crime against humanity.

The media also played a significant role by hosting interviews, allowing us to share our story to multitudes of audiences. These include a Channel 45 *The Good Life* station interview with host Barbara Beck in Orlando, Florida; The Riva & Secily *Real Living* show based in Central Florida; *Homekeepers,* a program with Arthelene Rippey in Clearwater, Florida; and an interview with Elaine Driscoll in Manchester, New Hampshire. Several local TV news stations in Florida aired reports on Run for Freedom, as well.

There was an awareness talk show broadcast from Titusville, Florida, as well as several broadcasts with radio station *WARV* in Providence, Rhode Island and radio station *Genesis 680 AM* in Tampa, Florida, which ran a two-hour documentary on Run for Freedom/ Human Trafficking on January 11, 2011, the National Human Trafficking Awareness Day.

Charisma Magazine published an article in March 2009; *Overflow Magazine* featured us as their cover story in July 2010; the official publication of the Assemblies of God, the *Pentecostal Evangel,* featured us in their February 2011 edition. There also have been many newspaper columns in several states that have interviewed us and reported on our awareness events. We are grateful for these and others who may have not been mentioned for helping us fight this terrible crime.

Would you believe me if I told you someone offered helicopter transportation to fly us anywhere in the state of Florida. Of course you would, after all these miracles you have read about. By the way, the color is a shiny metallic burnt *Orange*.

"One More" chapters in several states serve an important function in this army. Each chapter has a president, vice president, secretary/treasurer and volunteers who with much dedication and hard work raise awareness and funds in their own cities and communities.

This army has encouraged us greatly and strengthened and reinforced us financially. We are so grateful for monthly financial partners who faithfully give and the countless onetime donors who believe in the cause we are fighting for.

These stories reflect at least three things: First, God's heart breaks for *broken flowers* and so He uses people to make a difference. Second, many good, caring, loving and generous people exist in the world. Third, there is hope for innocent girls who have been victims of Sex Slavery.

The Run for Freedom story has had a divine and amazing beginning but my greatest dream is for it to have an ending; and that ending being the eradication of Sex Slavery in America.

Raising Awareness in America

When you think of the color Orange, what comes to your mind? If you are a professional or college football fan, most likely you would think of the Miami Dolphins, the Florida Gators or the University of Tennessee. If you or someone close to you has ever been incarcerated, the jump suit worn may have been Orange. You may even think of Florida oranges or orange juice. In the corporate business world's advertisements you would think of Home Depot or AT&T. Nature lovers would think of sunsets or harvest pumpkins in autumn. Construction workers know Orange represents safety. We all have something to associate with the color Orange. I would like to add to that context one more thing.

> Orange is the color of FREEDOM
> - freedom from Sex Slavery.

Have you ever asked why pink represents breast cancer awareness? The first known use of pink in connection with breast cancer awareness was in the fall of 1991, when the Susan G. Komen Foundation handed out pink ribbons to participants in its New York City race for breast cancer survivors. Then later it was adopted as the official symbol of National Breast Cancer Awareness.[1]

Orange for freedom goes back much further than 1991 – in fact, it goes back more than 320 years. Since 1690, people have been wearing Orange to represent their freedom.

The following article by Joshua Claybourn, *Wearing Orange on St. Patrick's Day*, will give you a brief history lesson. "Wearing green on St. Patrick's Day is not only widely practiced, it's virtually required. It's hard to imagine the holiday without green. But for a growing number of people, taking part in the fun means wearing Orange. According to this increasingly popular tradition, Protestants wear Orange, and the green clothing attire is worn by Catholics. Admittedly, this color tradition is not well known, but it has deep roots in Irish history. Some Protestant Irish have been known as the 'Orange Order' ever since 1690 when William of Orange (William III), the King of England, Scotland, and Ireland, defeated King James II, a Roman Catholic, in the Battle of the Boyne near Dublin. Although the 'Orange' in William's name actually referred to a province in southern France, the color reference stuck. This is why Orange now appears in the Irish flag – to symbolize the Protestant minority in Ireland.

"The Orange Order was founded on September 21, 1795 and it is perhaps the oldest still existing organization in Northern Ireland. The original purpose of the Orange Order is to bring together the Protestants of various denominations into one homogenous grouping to maintain their Protestant religion and way of life and as a distinctive affirmation that they intended to hold fast to the freedom of religion won at such a high cost at the Reformation." [2]

Run for Freedom launched the color Orange to represent freedom from Sex Slavery. In May 2008, a friend produced the first piece of awareness literature with Orange, and in September 2008 we provided orange bandanas for those who wanted to enlist in the army to help make a difference.

In this quest to raise awareness Run for Freedom sets up Orange tables with Orange products and literature on them. Every person who makes a donation/purchase becomes enlisted in our "Orange Army" to tell others they are wearing Orange for freedom from Sex Slavery.

The online store (runforfreedomstore.net) and the Orange table have a variety of items: our own designer neckties, shampoo and conditioner sets (directions on label say, "Lift up a prayer for victims to be set free"); our printed t-shirts, coffee tumblers, canvas bags, wristbands, pens; embroidered shirts, hats, hoodies, bandanas, sweatbands, scarves, earrings, and bracelets; and, of course, all items are Orange for freedom.

When I speak at men's gatherings across America, I talk about the part many of them play in the supply and demand of Sex Slavery. Whether knowingly or unknowingly their "purchases" have created emotional damage to these victims. But now they can reverse that process, change their lives; and by making a purchase from the Orange table and they can help provide emotional healing for residents at the Dream Home instead.

The broken flower on the cover of the book is an Orange gerbera daisy. When it blooms it brings beauty to its beholder. Fully grown it is six to eighteen inches in height with bright Orange blossoms and green leaves that curl up around the edges. It has long, thin, oval-shaped petals, which grow outward from the large, yellow/orange flower center. Birds, bees and butterflies are often attracted to it because of its brilliant coloring. An Orange gerbera daisy carries a specific meaning in the language of flowers established during the eighteenth century. Daisies are thought to express a message of innocence, gentleness, and youth. Bright Orange represents warmth, creativity, sunshine and happiness.[3]

I believe that there is hope for every young, innocent broken flower to have each of these things restored to her life.

Many people do not know that Sex Slavery still exists in the world. Some think that the trafficking of people for sexual exploitation only happens in countries outside America. Others who know it is in the United States may think that it is only in the large, heavily populated United States cities. Unfortunately, Sex Slavery has been documented in every state in America and takes place in every kind of community, in both urban and suburban areas. [4]

Run For Freedom knows that raising awareness in every community is necessary to eradicate Sex Slavery in America. If our justice system is going to make stiffer laws to put criminals behind bars throughout the United States, it will only come about as awareness is raised. Opening Dream Homes across America to help victims will only happen when good citizens with resources to help are made aware. Government funding will need to be allocated to train law enforcement, to educate school personnel, to establish task forces, and to establish residential housing. Only increased awareness will bring this about.

Several strides in awareness have been made over the last few years, even though we are just scratching the surface. Awareness will continue to grow through the printed page, including this book, newspapers, magazines, and other literature; media vehicles like talk shows, news reports, documentaries, and radio broadcasts; and through education, awareness events, and public speaking.

Run for Freedom organizes a variety of events in the country including 5K's, motorcycle rides, banquets, sports tournaments, and Dinner and a Movie events. These happen through the local "One More" chapters who are passionate about raising awareness and fighting Sex Slavery. This is a great way for everyone to get involved with Run for Freedom's mission all over the United States. We look forward to the day when all fifty states are represented.

It is planned to offer college level courses online as part of the future Run For Freedom University. These courses will focus on the origin of American white Sex Slavery, right up to modern day slavery. The objectives for the students are to present a case for the urgency of raising awareness of Sex Slavery in America; to give attention to the history of the traffic of foreign girls into America and the traffic of American girls to other countries; to become acquainted with the process of recovery for victims rescued out of Sex Slavery; to become familiar with the relevant laws, immigration, law enforcement, and the need for social and spiritual justice; to understand the global impact Sex Slavery has on the financial industry and on the criminal market; to create a passion that reaches out to victims, perpetrators, and the slave owners; to develop the student's ability to be proactive in spotting a victim, raising awareness, and working with victims in a residential setting; and to recognize that in every dark situation good people have been and always will be agents of divine hope.

In America, an average of 2,185 children are being reported missing each day.[5] It is estimated annually that nearly 300,000 American youth are at risk of becoming victims of commercial sexual exploitation.[6] The majority of American victims of commercial sexual exploitation tend to be runaway or thrown away youth who live on the streets. These children generally come from homes of abuse or abandonment. The majority of girls engaged in formal prostitution are pimp controlled. Commercial sexual exploitation of children is linked to escort and massage services; private dancing, drinking, and photographic clubs; major sporting and recreational events; major cultural events; and conventions, modeling agencies, and tourist destinations.[7]

The National Center for Missing and Exploited Children states that the typical entry age for sexual exploitation is 12 to 14 for girls, and 11 to 13 for boys.

While I was in Wesley Chapel, Florida, to speak on Sex Slavery, the pastor introduced us as "Champions of the Pennies". He alluded to how pennies are stepped on, stepped over, forgotten, and forsaken. I was so inspired by his words I later penned the following.

We are all familiar with the penny, the one-cent piece in our currency, but how many remember penny candy? When I was a young child I went to a store called Iron's Market. It was just around the corner from where I lived, so I visited often. You could buy almost everything for a penny and some items were two for a penny. Finding a penny walking home from school was a treat for any kid, because pennies had worth and value but today it's a different story.

Pennies now live lives of rejection. When seen on the ground they are ignored and not given a second glance. They are thought to be no longer good for anything, worthless, often kicked to the curb, dropped and forgotten. Many folks actually consider the penny a nuisance. We step on them, walk over them, or if they are noticed at all we won't even bend over to pick one up. That is considered too much trouble for just a penny. When receiving change some say, "Keep it; I don't need it." We skip over the penny to the nickels, dimes, and quarters.

The United States Treasury is talking about retiring the penny, putting it to rest even though it has been with us since 1793. It costs the U.S. Mint 1.7 cents to make a penny, 70% more than the value of the coin. Since 1982 the copper penny is no longer copper other than the 2.5% plating, and the other 97.5% is zinc. [8]

The coin's demise is evident at convenience stores where you can "take one or leave one" in the penny tray. It is the least valued coin. That fact that it is useless, ignored, discarded, and rejected is likely how victims of Sex Slavery must feel after they have been treated terribly.

Jesus said, "When you feed the hungry or give a drink to the thirsty or visit the sick or those doing time in prison remember whatever you do for the least of them it is the same as doing it to Me." The least of them – that sounds like the penny, doesn't it?

Just as there are more pennies in existence than any other coin, there are a lot of rejected people all around us. They all have value and importance no matter what anyone says or thinks.

Every "penny," or person, has the right to know God, and sometimes because they have been forgotten, they think God has forgotten them as well.

I have a small coin collection of Indian head pennies, steel pennies made during World War II, and wheat pennies; and they all have value. I would never step on them or discard them.

Do you collect pennies? I want to encourage you to be His hands extended and become a penny collector. You will find those who have been tarnished, scratched, dented, and worn out. They are waiting to be valued, picked up and held tightly.

On June 22, 2007 the Senate established the **National Day of Human Trafficking Awareness** to be observed on January 11. This represents one of the many examples of the ongoing commitment of the United States to raise awareness and to actively oppose human trafficking.

The United States has long been a leader in the advancement of human rights, and our countrymen and countrywomen are committed to protecting individual freedom. We, as Americans, believe that it is wrong to participate in any form of human trafficking. We understand that in order to fight human trafficking in every part of our society, we have to make everyone in our communities aware of how damaging this industry is to our infrastructure, and we must be dedicated to stopping it. It is not about politics or religion or race or gender – we simply cannot accept a world where slavery exists in any form.[9]

Run for Freedom is dreaming about a National Orange for Freedom Day in conjunction with the National Human Trafficking Awareness Day when Americans everywhere will join together to wear Orange and proclaim freedom from Sex Slavery.

8 Dream Homes Across America

I am exhilarated when I think about a Dream Home residential facility filled with former victims of Sex Slavery beginning their process to be made whole. I also think about clothing, food, education, life skills, job training and qualified staff. I think about law enforcement, transportation, court hearings, health issues, medical care, dental care, and the possibility of pregnancy and sexually transmitted diseases. I think about the girls who may have trouble sleeping or may not want to wake up. I think about the drugs and alcohol used to numb their memories. I think about eating disorders and psychological and sexual abuse counseling. I think about their feelings of pain, rejection, fear, anger, and shame. I think about the language barriers, social disorders, and learning disabilities. I think about the ones who may want to return to the life from which they came, and the ones who will never go back. Most of all I think about God's power working through loving professionals to transform a life of despair into something beautiful.

What comes to your mind when you think of a Dream Home? Perhaps you see a mansion with a spacious driveway, a flower garden, lots of formal rooms, several fireplaces, and ample bedrooms, and bathrooms? Or perhaps you see a courtyard trimmed with elm trees and a Roman swimming pool with all the outdoor amenities? Or you may picture a rustic ranch home with lots of wide-open space, surrounded by scenic breathtaking mountains, roaming cattle, grazing horses, fresh air, and breathtaking starry nights?

I would picture an old Victorian home with a copper roof, wrap-around porch, separate servant quarters, cozy rooms, and a boat garage on a peninsular on the east coast of Maine. The whispering fog and the smell of the sea would surely feel like home. Its private beach and the sound of crashing waves would make a perfect setting for each new sunrise.

The first Run for Freedom Dream Home is actually a picturesque New England-style home nestled among oak trees and vibrantly colored bushes and flowers.

The home is on multiple acres with a private spring fed lake, white sand beach, and a screened in dock. Fishing and boating are always available at your slightest whim. A gazebo is set in a tranquil woodsy area. There is a vegetable garden and a wonderful orchard with orange, grapefruit, tangerine, lemon, plum, persimmon, peach, nectarine, pear, loquat, and even pomegranate trees. To top it off there are rare muscadine grape vines.

The property features a three-stall barn to house horses and goats, and separate lodging for the caretaker. Huge oaks majestically protect the grounds, and the sunset on the water is a sight to see! The two-story home has plentiful natural light inside, soaring tongue and groove ceilings, a stone fireplace, real pinewood floors, and huge front and back porches with rocking chairs. There are two dorm rooms, two bedrooms, and five bathrooms. The chapel/learning center has two sliding doors that overlook the lake, and the fragrance of jasmine permeates the nearby trellises in season. It's a place where the presence of God is.

There was no home available for one survivor named **Zinnia**. She was a broken flower who has now blossomed into a beautiful woman. What follows are her own words.

"I escaped the sex industry for the last time in 1998, and as miserable as the process had been it was not an easy exit. I was caught up in the complicated criminal justice system. I was embarrassed and ashamed to be stigmatized not only as a whore but also a criminal. I was desperately tired, alone and afraid that my life was over and that I would never amount to anything.

"I had a low-grade drug addiction and an even lower self-esteem. There were and still are countless flashes from the life that refuse to let go of me. I sought professional help but to no avail. I made several feeble attempts at suicide by over-dosing on pills that left me numb and only more disappointed

that I failed. I wondered why I had made so many bad choices and spent each day regretting my life. I sought out new love relationships that only added to my misery.

"I didn't grow up with all this despondent and self-destructive behavior. My parents were protective and supportive. I was the oldest child of a respected pastor. I was an avid reader and did relatively well in school.

"At 14 years old I was fascinated with the concepts of, 'Having It All,' and, 'Women Who Run With The Wolves.' I began to question God and His existence.

"I was absorbed into the eat-or-be-eaten philosophy that seems to be the axis upon which the secular money driven world turns. I enjoyed hanging out in nightclubs, cavorting with drug dealers, musicians, bikers, lawyers, doctors, firemen, police officers, and even an FBI agent. I made huge money. I could sell anything, and I discovered that performance based pay plans gave me the opportunity to earn as much money as I wanted. A friend suggested I try out cocktail waitressing at a strip club, and for whatever convoluted reason that seemed to make sense. Quick cash was not only a necessity; it became the golden cow I could never get enough of.

"It took very little time for my life to spiral downward into late nights, considerable drinking, recreational drug use and one-night stands. I was recklessly 'running with the wolves.' The men I stayed with encouraged my entrepreneurial attitude towards making money with my good looks, charm and by selling sex.

"I found my way out of the life several times but always fell back in. I was in a perpetual state of self-induced confusion. I had no fear and very few boundaries. Towards the end I was depressed and very tired. I had shut down my ability to feel for so long that I was emotionless and very empty inside. My life was a roller coaster of thrilling highs and devastating lows. I didn't trust anyone, and the shame and guilt and the feelings of worthlessness were overwhelming to me. After ten years, unless something changed I was done. I quietly and without a lot of fanfare asked God to save me from myself, *and I promised I would find a way to pay Him back.*

"There were no fireworks, but God did indeed go to work and began to bring new people into my life that would bring me the gifts of real love and forgiveness. I began to heal, and many things were becoming new. Then, after a few years, an incredible man who accepted me came into my life, and we married. Soon the desire came along to help other girls who had been trapped in this life, as well. I shared my story with other girls, teaching, finding resources, and being an advocate. The only piece that was missing was a safe home. I joyfully discovered that Run For Freedom had established the first Dream Home in Florida for female victims of Sex Slavery."

The purchase of the Dream Home was a miracle. I put together a list of eight properties and off we went one day with a realtor friend. She offered to pass on her commission for the cause – one of the first of many blessings!

The first property we looked at had multiple buildings and all the bells and whistles. Then we saw a few more; one too small, the other too close to the road, and the other was priced too high. Then we went to the fifth property on the list.

As soon as we drove onto the property and got out of the car, a sweet and gentle horse greeted us with a nudge and followed us all around the lovely grounds. We were amazed, having already planned to include equine therapy in the program. Once we opened the front door, we felt the warmth of the design and caught a glimpse of the back yard; we rushed out a side door. As we rounded the curve of the house and saw the lake and more beautiful landscaping, we knew immediately this was going to be the Dream Home.

We looked around some more and told our realtor friend we were sold. She suggested we continue on with our list of houses to see, in light of the fact that it was a short sale and could take a long time, if it even went through at all. We knew that a realtor set the price of $399,000, and that there was over $690,000 owed to the bank.

We were sure we didn't need to look at any more properties because anything else would simply pale in comparison.

> By faith we believed that this property was going to be the first Dream Home in America.

The bank later foreclosed and listed the property for sale. We ended up going to contract within 30 days. We made a $5,000 deposit; the bank set the closing date for 40 days later by which time we would need an additional $278,000. If you did the math you will note we purchased the home for $282,000 not the $399,000 price, and certainly not for the $690,000 owed to the bank. I believe because God's heart is broken over His "daughters" who are used and abused, He worked another miracle!

The Run for Freedom Dream Home's objective is to help the resident re-enter society as a healthy, whole, productive person. The program includes but is not limited to: housing, food, medical care, life skills, education, General Education Development classes, English as a second language, counseling and mentoring, work skills training, and therapy animals. Spiritual healing through Bible curriculum, chapel services, prayer, and meditation are offered as well.

The Dream Home is a one-month, three-month, twelve-month (or as long as it takes) faith based program for young women who are rescued out of Sex Slavery. Each situation is tailored to their specific needs. The goal is to provide them with effective and comprehensive solutions in order to become mentally and emotionally balanced, as well as physically and spiritually whole, to becoming happy, productive members of society.

Recovery from Sex Slavery is a lifelong endeavor and we are committed to give a lifetime of support.

The overall objective of the program is to initiate a total change in values and lifestyle by applying life skills, education, and biblical principles to their lives. We will use trained, capable staff who live on the premises to insure an atmosphere of warmth, trust, and support.

The Dream Home Program offers a variety of job training opportunities for the students:

Jewelry Design - Professional jewelry designers teach the students how to express themselves creatively. They find serenity and joy completing artistically designed pieces they can be proud of and that bring in revenue for the Dream Home on the Orange product table.

Horticulture - This portion of the program will enable the students to learn how to cultivate and grow fruits, vegetables, herbs, and flowers. It develops another line of business expertise and job training, while at the same time producing emotional serenity and therapy.

Equine Therapy - Trust and emotional bonding play a significant role in this program. Horses provide therapeutic healing as the students voluntarily interact with them.

Office - This provides training in office skills to prepare the students to interact professionally with the public workforce.

Kitchen - The students learn teamwork as they prepare daily meals for the home, and learn through cooking, baking, meal planning, following shopping tips, and serving others.

Broken Flowers

Here's another story about a girl named **Iris,** whose "daddy" pimp forced her to have as many as twenty clients a day.

> She had to achieve a dollar value quota or risked being punished or threatened.

Then one day she heard about the Dream Home and decided to run for her freedom. After a twelve day stay, she went back to the streets, but this time something was different. She began to think about the Dream Home and its loving staff. The contrast of the two environments began to work on her.

Two weeks later she ran again, bought a bus ticket and headed to see her family. While on the way she threw her high heel working shoes out the window signifying she was done with her pimp and her life as a sex worker. Iris soon contacted the Dream Home, and when asked what was different this time she said that she needed a second chance because it could possibly be her last chance. She also said being around her family changed her. She was afraid that if she didn't return to the Dream Home for ninety days or longer she might end up going back to "the life" and perhaps even end up dead. She wanted to get her driver's license, earn her GED, and learn a trade to get a decent job. She also wanted a deeper spiritual life, to grow closer to God, and to be able to love herself. She said she knew it was the best thing for her life. Yes, she came back, obtained her driver's license, accepted Jesus as her Savior, and is pursuing her GED.

Every girl who has been robbed of her purity and freedom as a sex slave needs to have the same opportunity as Iris. The opportunity to go to a place where she can grow, flourish and become a woman who is productive, healthy, and whole.

My desire is to see Dream Homes established across America. Hopefully this book has touched your heart, and you will want to engage in this fight with us. Maybe you have the resources or the ability to raise finances to open a Dream Home in your area. What has been done in Florida is both sustainable and reproducible. Together we can make a difference by rescuing one girl at a time and helping her develop into a radiant gerber flower!

Conclusion

To win this fight against Sex Slavery in America it will take every one of us doing our part: federal, state, and local law enforcement; the judicial system, religious institutions, and colleges and universities; students, social workers, medical professionals, and human trafficking activists; and American citizens of every ethnicity, gender, and age.

Thus far, my travels across America have been encouraging. I have met thousands of people who are passionate to see *broken flowers* set free and made whole. Many are wearing Orange, proclaiming freedom and raising awareness at every opportunity. At the same time I have been discouraged with America's pop culture media that has desensitized the populace and glamorized pimping and prostitution. This breakdown of society's morals opens the doorway to accept the commercial sex trade as the norm. No thought is given to where these sex slaves come from or who they are as individuals.

The Internet had become the main culprit in connecting sex slaves with clients. As long as online sites are permitted to place sex advertisements, the struggle for moral decency and the victimization of young innocent girls will continue.

On September 3, 2010 Craigslist (some have called it an "online pimp") was forced to terminate its popular sex advertisements in the United States. An average advertisement costs $10, and the revenue loss was twelve million to fifteen million dollars. Federal law protects Craigslist against liability for what its users post. Yet, it is well known that it promotes Sex Slavery and other terrible crimes. With Craigslist's 10,000 daily sex advertisements gone, many other websites have come to the forefront. It was reported that approximately ten websites anticipated an estimated $63 million in sex advertisement revenue in the United States in 2010. Backpage.com, operated by Village Voice Media, expected an estimated $17.5 million in online sex advertising in 2010. [1]

Presently, it is estimated that there are 49 countries trafficking into 91 cities in America.[2] There are American girls trafficked within our country, as well as reverse trafficking where our girls are sent to other countries. All of them become human merchandise, property of some trafficker, pimp or madam. They are in massage parlors, spas, escort services, strip clubs, on the web or working the streets.

Run for Freedom took a team of people to Orlando, Florida to engage with prostituted girls who are working the streets. Our purpose was to build trust and to offer the Dream Home program as an option. Prior to going we held a training meeting to better prepare the team and when it was over someone handed me a penny that they had found. I put it in my pocket and asked God to let it represent someone I would meet that day; a person that needed to be reached.

Once out on the streets I saw **Hyacinth** and **Lilac,** obviously dressed for work. Men driving by were blowing horns, shouting sexual innuendoes and one guy was even half hanging out of his vehicle as he passed by. This behavior appeared typical to the girls and did not seem to alarm them in any way.

As another team member and myself intentionally walked past the girls, I casually said, "Hi girls, how are you doing?" They responded with a perky, "Doing good." Once ahead of them we stopped and waited for them to get closer. As they approached I handed them a card with a phone number on it and asked, "Have you ever thought about getting out of the life?" Hyacinth answered saying, "I just told Lilac that I prayed to God and asked him to send someone to help me get out of the life." I asked, "You said that just now, while walking?" "Yes", she replied. I asked Lilac, "What did you respond when Hyacinth said that?" And she replied, "I want the same thing." I said, "Here I am, God sent me to help you get out." I then asked them their names and told them that there was a safe house in Central Florida. *This really grabbed their attention!* I asked them if they would like to meet a friend of mine who was with us and had been out of the life for 12 years. They agreed to change directions and come with us. As we walked I asked Hyacinth, "If you were out of the life tell me some things you would want to do?" She answered, "Get my driver's license, get my GED, and get trained for a good job because I have kids." Once they were introduced to Zinnia we talked further and told them what to expect when they decide to call us for help. We gave them a cold bottle of water and a bag containing personal products along with a spiritual note card.

Before long, Lilac, who had walked across the street, was whisked away by a customer in a truck.

Nine days later Hyacinth called to start the process to run for her freedom and find new life through the Dream Home Program.

Slavery must be eradicated; it is an evil that is stealing innocence and purity from our girls. On December 6, 1865, the United States Congress adopted the Thirteenth Amendment to the Constitution officially abolishing slavery in America.

We must fight for these *broken flowers* and not stop until we win. Ecclesiastes 3:1 states, "There is a time for everything, and a season for every activity under the heavens." I believe it is time to speak for those who cannot speak for themselves.

It is time to boldly proclaim FREEDOM for everyone.

It is time for the church to engage in the battle with God's power and make a difference.

It is time to eradicate Sex Slavery in our community, our city, our state, and our country.

God bless you!

Words Defined

Advocacy: Efforts to influence public policy and resource allocation decisions within political, economic, and social systems and institutions.

Bitch: The most common term used by pimps when referring to a prostitute.

Brothel: An establishment or place specifically dedicated to prostitution.

Branding: To burn with a hot iron on the skin or to place a tattoo on a victim indicating ownership by a trafficker or pimp.

Commercial Sex: Any sex act including exotic dancing, massages, or pornography that is performed for financial gain.

Coyote: One who illegally smuggles people across borders of countries.

Cyber Sex (Also known as computer or Internet sex): A virtual sex encounter in which two or more people connect online verbally and/or visually.

Daddy: A term of endearment for a pimp.

Debt Bondage: When a person is held as collateral to work off their debt. Yet while being held, they fall increasingly deeper in debt, creating an endless cycle of bondage.

Escort/Call Girl: Sex worker not necessarily visible to the general public.

Exotic Dancer: One who works in a strip club – to perform on stage or for private lap dances. They are encouraged to sell liquor to clients and are paid solely by tips from bar patrons. They are expected to pay house fees known as "tip outs." This is considered the "gateway drug" for prostitution.

Ho: A common slang term for a prostitute.

Hooker: A prostitute. Note: originally known as "Hooker's Girls." This term started in the civil war when General Hooker of the Union Army (known as the first pimp) tried to protect his troops from Venereal Disease by buying the healthiest girls and pimping them to his corps of 20,000 men.

John: A common slang term for a man who pays for the services of a prostitute.

Madam: A woman who owns or runs a brothel.

Money Laundering: The practice of engaging in financial transactions to conceal the identity, source, and/or destination of illegally gained money and/or when the proceeds of a crime are converted into assets, which appear to have a legitimate origin.

Pander: To facilitate or provide a prostitute for a customer.

Pimp: A man who gains income by procuring and managing prostitutes with permission and/or force.

Pimp Stick: Any type of item (weapon or tool) used by a pimp to beat his prostitute.

Prostitute: One who is paid to provide sexual acts.

Seasoning: The process of breaking a victim's spirit and gaining control over them, using rapes, beatings, brandings, manipulation and intimidation. Note: there is actually a manual for pimps on how to season victims.

Sex Trafficking: A modern-day form of slavery in which a commercial sex act is induced by force, fraud, or coercion.

Slavery: Involuntary subjection to another or others. It emphasizes the idea of complete ownership and control by a master. Note: Slavery is not legal in any country in the world.

Stable: The term for a pimp's group of prostitutes.

Streetwalker: A prostitute who solicites sex by walking the street or standing on a street corner.

Trick: A slang term for sex performed by a prostitute.

Works Cited

Endnotes

1. "Trafficking in Persons Report 2009 Major Forms of Trafficking in Persons." U.S. Department of State. N.p., n.d. Web. 9 June 2011. <http://www.state.gov/g/tip/rls/tiprpt/2009/123126.htm>.

Introduction

1. "What Is Human Trafficking." United Nations Office on Drugs and Crime. N.p., n.d. Web. 9 June 2011. <http://www.unodc.org/unodc/en/human-trafficking/what-is-human-trafficking.html>.

2. "The Campaign to Rescue & Restore Victims of Human Trafficking: About Human Trafficking." Administration for Children and Families Home Page. N.p., 10 Aug. 2010. Web. 9 June 2011. <http://www.acf.hhs.gov/trafficking/about/index.html>.

3. "Trafficking in Persons Report 2007." U.S. Department of State. N.p., n.d. Web. 9 June 2011. <http://www.state.gov/g/tip/rls/tiprpt/2007/>.

4. Bruggeman, Jean , and Elizabeth Keyes. "Meeting the Legal Needs of Human Trafficking Victims." American Bar Association, n.d. Web. 9 June 2011. <www.americanbar.org/content/dam/aba/migrated/domviol/pdfs/DV_Trafficking.authcheckdam.pdf>.

5. "Sex Slavery: Woman/Women Trafficking, Sexual Trafficking, Human Sex Trafficking: - Soroptimist International." Women Organization (Women Volunteer): International Women's Organization for Womens Issues - Soroptimist International. n.d. Web. 9 June 2011. <http://www.soroptimist.org/trafficking/trafficking.html>.

6. Genesis 1:26

7. "Polaris Project I Polaris Project I Combating Human Trafficking and Modern-day Slavery." Polaris Project I Combating Human Trafficking and Modern-day Slavery. N.p., n.d. Web. 9 June 2011. <http://www.polarisproject.org/about-us/introduction>.

8. Williamson, Erin, Nicole Dutch, and Heather Clawson Caliber.

"Evidence-Based Mental Health Treatment for Victims of Human Trafficking: Main Page." Office of the Assistant Secretary for Planning and Evaluation, HHS. N.p., n.d. Web. 9 June 2011. <http://aspe.hhs.gov/hsp/07/humantrafficking/mentalhealth/index. shtml>.

8. Trafficking in Persons Report 2007.

Chapter 1

1. Roe, Clifford Griffith, and B. S. Steadwell. The great war on white slavery, or, Fighting for the protection of our girls truthful and chaste account of the hideous trade of buying and selling young girls for immoral purposes .... U.S.: s.n.], 1911. Print.

2. "Traffic-in-Souls - Trailer - Cast - Showtimes - NYTimes.com ." Movie Reviews, Showtimes and Trailers - Movies - New York Times - The New York Times. N.p., n.d. Web. 14 June 2011. <http:// movies.nytimes.com/movie/50688/Traffic-in-Souls/overview>.

3. Roe.

4. "Project Rescue - Frequently Asked Questions." Project Rescue - Home. N.p., n.d. Web. 14 June 2011. <http://www.projectrescue. com/faqs.html>.

5. Roe.

6. Hendley, Matthew. "Prostitutes Plan to Profit Big From Super Bowl Week in South Florida - Broward/Palm Beach News - The Daily Pulp." Broward Palm Beach Blogs. N.p., 30 Jan. 2010. Web. 14 June 2011. <http://blogs.browardpalmbeach.com/ pulp/2010/01/prostitutes_super_bowl_south_florida.php>.

Chapter 2

1. Sheidlower, Jesse. "A brief history of the verb to pimp. - By Jesse Sheidlower - Slate Magazine." Slate Magazine. N.p., 11 Feb. 2010. Web. 16 June 2011. <http://www.slate.com/id/2184211/>.

2. Farley, Melissa. "About Prostitution Research & Education." Prostitution Research & Education Website. N.p., 2 Apr. 2000. Web. 10 Aug. 2011. <http://www.prostitutionresearch.com/ factsheet.html>.

3. Bell, Rachael. "Gary Leon Ridgway The Green River Serial Killer" A Nightmare Come True" Crime Library on truTV.com." truTV.com: Not Reality. Actuality.. N.p., n.d. Web. 16 June 2011. <http://www. trutv.com/library/crime/serial_killers/predators/greenriver/ routine_2.html>.

4. "Prostitution - Wikipedia, the free encyclopedia." Wikipedia, the free encyclopedia. N.p., n.d. Web. 16 June 2011. <http://en.wikipedia. org/wiki/Prostitution#cite_note-18>.

5. Allen, Ernie . "Ernie Allen Testimony on Domestic Minor Sex Trafficking to the U.S. House of Representatives Subcommittee on Crime, Terrorism and Homeland Security Committee on the Judiciary." National Center for Missing and Exploited Children. N.p., n.d. Web. 16 June 2011. <http://www.missingkids.com/ missingkids/servlet/NewsEventServlet?LanguageCountry= en_US&PageId=4339>.

6. McCall, Andrew. The medieval underworld . London: H. Hamilton, 1979. Print.

7. Kironde, Lusuga. "Daily News I The growing incidence of prostitution in Urban areas." Daily News I The leading Online news edition in Tanzania. N.p., 23 Oct. 2010. Web. 16 June 2011. <http://www. dailynews.co.tz/columnist/?n=14012&cat=columnist>.

8. "Sexwork Cyber Resource Center II Welcome." Sexwork Cyber Resource Center II Welcome. N.p., n.d. Web. 16 June 2011. <http://www.sexwork.com/>.

9. "Deadwood Magazine - The Girls Raid!." Deadwood Magazine - History, News, Photos and Features from the American Frontier. N.p., n.d. Web. 16 June 2011. <http://www.deadwoodmagazine. com/archivedsite/Archives/Girls_Raid.htm>.

10. "Rhode Island Outlaws Indoor Prostitution, Closing Legal Loophole - Prostitution - ProCon.org." Prostitution ProCon.org -- Should prostitution be legal?. N.p., 4 Nov. 2009. Web. 16 June 2011. <http://prostitution.procon.org/view.additional r esource.php?resourceID=003297>.

11. "Prostitution - Wikipedia, the free encyclopedia." Wikipedia, the free

encyclopedia. N.p., n.d. Web. 20 June 2011. <http://en.wikipedia. org/wiki/Prostitution>.

12. "Violence against prostitutes - Wikipedia, the free encyclopedia." Wikipedia, the free encyclopedia. N.p., n.d. Web. 16 June 2011. <http://en.wikipedia.org/wiki/Violence_against_prostitutes#cite_note-0>.

13. Bell.

14. Farley, Melissa. "Prostitution Harms Women Even if Indoors." Violence Against Women. SAFE Publications, n.d. Web. 16 June 2011. <www.prostitutionresearch.com/Farley%20Indoor%20 Prostitution.pdf>.

15. "Prostitution laws: health risks and hypocrisy -- 171 (2): 109 -- Canadian Medical Association Journal." Canadian Medical Association Journal - June 16, 2011. N.p., 20 July 2004. Web. 16 June 2011. <http://www.cmaj.ca/cgi/content/full/171/2/109?maxto show=&hits=25&RESULTFORMAT=&fulltext=prostitution&search id=1&FIRSTINDEX=0&sortspec=date&resourcetype=HWCIT>.

16. Farley.

17. "US v. Pipkins, 378 F. 3d 1281 - Court of Appeals, 11th Circuit 2004." Google Scholar. N.p., 2 Aug. 2004. Web. 16 June 2011. <http:// scholar.google.com/scholar_case?case=1303352174754989479 &hl=en&as_sdt=2&as_vis=1&oi=scholarr>.

18. Ibid.

19. Ibid.

20. Rowe, Claudia. "No way out: Teen girls sell bodies in Seattle - seattlepi.com." Seattle news, sports, events, entertainment I seattlepi.com - seattlepi.com. N.p., 26 June 2008. Web. 16 June 2011. <http://www.seattlepi.com/default/article/No-way-out-Teen- girls-sell-bodies-in-Seattle-1277746.php>.

21. "Pimp - Wikipedia, the free encyclopedia." Wikipedia, the free encyclopedia. N.p., n.d. Web. 10 Aug. 2011. <http://en.wikipedia. org/wiki/Pimp>.

22. Raymond, Janice G., Donna M. Hughes, and Carol Gomez. Sex trafficking of women in the United States: international and domestic trends. Kingston, R.I.: Coalition Against Trafficking in Women, 2001. Print.

Chapter 3

1. Ropelato, Jerry. " Internet Pornography Statistics - TopTenReviews." Internet Filter Software Review 2011 | Best Internet Filter | Block Pornography – TopTenReviews. N.p., n.d. Web. 17 June 2011. <http://internet-filter-review.toptenreviews.com/internet-pornography-statistics.html>.

2. Reporter, IBTimes. "Playboy accepts Hugh Hefner's sweetened bid, publisher to go private - Entertainment & Stars." International Business News, Financial News, Market News, Politics, Forex, Commodities - International Business Times - IBTimes. com. N.p., 10 Jan. 2011. Web. 17 June 2011. <http://www. ibtimes.com/articles/99269/20110110/playboy-accepts-hugh-hefner-s-sweetened-bid-publisher-to-go-private.htm>.

3. Ropelato.

4. Ibid.

5. Ibid.

6. Young, Kimberly S. Internet Addiction: The Emergence of a New Clinical Disorder. Bradford, Pennsylvania: Kimberly S. Young., 1998. Print.

7. Tomiuc, Eugen. "World: Interpol Official Discusses Human Trafficking, Internet Pornography." GlobalSecurity.org - Reliable Security Information. N.p., n.d. Web. 17 June 2011. <http://www. globalsecurity.org/security/library/news/2003/05/sec-030514-rfel-142137.htm>.

8. "Internet Pornography Statistics." Kid Safe Internet | Kids Online Browser. N.p., n.d. Web. 17 June 2011. <http://www. mykidsbrowser.com/internet-pornography-statistics.php>.

9. "International Trafficking | Polaris Project | Combating Human Trafficking and Modern-day Slavery." Polaris Project | Combating

Human Trafficking and Modern-day Slavery. N.p., n.d. Web. 17 June 2011. <http://www.polarisproject.org/human-trafficking/international-trafficking>.

10. "1893 Chicago Worlds Fair." City Life. N.p., n.d. Web. 17 June 2011. <http://www1.cuny.edu/portal_ur/content/citylife/world.php>.

11. "Street Prostitution I Polaris Project I Combating Human Trafficking and Modern-day Slavery." Polaris Project I Combating Human Trafficking and Modern-day Slavery. N.p., n.d. Web. 17 June 2011. <http://www.polarisproject.org/human-trafficking/sex-trafficking-in-the-us/street-prostitution>.

12. "Former Sex Slave Gives Students Insight - Jacksonville News Story - WJXT Jacksonville." News 4 Jax I Jacksonville News, Jacksonville, Florida News, Weather, Sports I WJXT Channel 4. N.p., 22 Oct. 2010. Web. 17 June 2011. <http://www.news4jax.com/news/25478775/detail.html>.

13. Landesman, Peter. "The Girls Next Door - Sidebar - NYTimes.com." The New York Times - Breaking News, World News & Multimedia. N.p., 25 Jan. 2004. Web. 17 June 2011. <http://www.nytimes.com/2004/01/25/magazine/25SEXTRAFFIC.html>.

Chapter 4

1. Human Trafficking. Dir. Christian Duguay. Perf. Mira Sorvino, Donald Sutherland, Rémy Girard. Echo Bridge Home Entertainment, 2006. DVD.

2. Flores, Theresa L., and PeggySue Wells. The slave across the street: the true story of how an American teen survived the world of human trafficking. Boise, ID: Ampelon Pub., 2010. Print.

3. "Modern Slavery 101." iAbolish.org I American Anti-Slavery Group. N.p., n.d. Web. 17 June 2011. <http://www.iabolish.org/index.php?option=com_content&view=category&layout=blog&id=4&Itemid=7>.

4. Herrera, Consuelo. "Sex Slavery and its link to money laundering - Accounting." BellaOnline -- The Voice of Women. N.p., n.d. Web. 17 June 2011. <http://www.bellaonline.com/articles/art53836.asp>.

5. Ibid.

6. Freedman, Michael. "Fantasy Island - Forbes.com." Information for the World's Business Leaders - Forbes.com. N.p., 24 Apr. 2006. Web. 17 June 2011. <http://www.forbes.com/ forbes/2006/0424/090.html>.

7. "Human Trafficking and migrant smuggling." Social Pathology in Modern World. N.p., 17 Nov. 2010. Web. 17 June 2011. <http:// sivanandammsw.blogspot.com/2010/11/human-trafficking-and-migrant-smuggling.html>.

8. "Human trafficking - Wikipedia, the free encyclopedia." Wikipedia, the free encyclopedia. N.p., n.d. Web. 17 June 2011. <http:// en.wikipedia.org/wiki/Human_trafficking#cite_note-61>.

9. "Internet Pornography Statistics." My Kids Browser. N.p., n.d. Web. 17 June 2011. <www.mykidsafeinternet.com/pornography_stats. php>.

10. "Snopes.com: Snuff Films." snopes.com: Urban Legends Reference Pages. N.p., n.d. Web. 17 June 2011. <http://www.snopes.com/ horrors/madmen/snuff.asp>.

11. Landesman, Peter. "The Girls Next Door - NYTimes.com." NY Times Advertisement. N.p., 25 June 2004. Web. 20 June 2011. <http:// www.nytimes.com/2004/01/25/magazine/the-girls-next-door. html>.

12. Nasaw, Daniel. " New Jersey mayors and rabbis arrested in corruption and money laundering investigation I World news I guardian.co.uk ." Latest news, comment and reviews from the Guardian I guardian.co.uk . N.p., 23 July 2009. Web. 17 June 2011. <http://www.guardian.co.uk/world/2009/jul/23/new-jersey-corruption-money-laundering>.

13. "Dealing with Organized Crime in Scotland." Scottish Crime and Drug Enforcement Agency . N.p., n.d. Web. 17 June 2011. <www.sdea.police.uk/SDEA-Annual-Report/SCDEA%20 Annual%20Report%2007-08.pdf>.

Chapter 5

1. "Statistics and Information - Human Trafficking Awareness Coalition in Sarasota County ." Human Trafficking Awareness Coalition in Sarasota County - HTAC. N.p., n.d. Web. 17 June 2011. <http://htsrq.weebly.com/statistics-and-information.html>.

2. "Child Prostitution I Streetlight PHX." Streetlight PHX. N.p., 30 Mar. 2011. Web. 17 June 2011. <http://streetlightphx.com/tag/child-prostitution/>.

3. "Abolish Slavery!." Don't Trade Lives. N.p., n.d. Web. 17 June 2011. <www.fmwm.org/cms_media/files/AbolishSlaveryWorldVision.pdf>.

4. "Pimp - Wikipedia, the free encyclopedia." Wikipedia, the free encyclopedia. N.p., n.d. Web. 17 June 2011. <http://en.wikipedia.org/wiki/Pimp#cite_note-12>.

5. "Debt Bondage and Trafficking in Women." Home . N.p., 1 Sept. 2005. Web. 17 June 2011. <http://stopvaw.org/Debt_Bondage_and_Trafficking_in_Women.html>.

6. Farlow, Rita. "Search warrant says ex-Clearwater fire chief videotaped sex with girl - St. Petersburg Times." Tampa, Florida newspapers: The Times & tbt* I Powering tampabay.com. N.p., 18 Dec. 2010. Web. 17 June 2011. <http://www.tampabay.com/news/publicsafety/crime/search-warrant-says-ex-clearwater-fire-chief-videotaped-sex-with-girl/1140607>.

7. "Girl Forced Into Prostitution; Couple Gets Probation - News Story - WFTV Orlando." Orlando News, Central Florida News, Daytona Beach News, Melbourne FL News, Weather, Traffic, Sports - WFTV Channel 9. N.p., 20 Aug. 2010. Web. 17 June 2011. <http://www.wftv.com/news/24702705/detail.html>.

8. "William Wilberforce Trafficking Victims Protection Reauthorization Act of 2008." Welcome to Travel.State.Gov. N.p., n.d. Web. 17 June 2011. <http://travel.state.gov/visa/laws/telegrams/telegrams_4542.html>.

Chapter 7

1. "Breast Cancer Pink I Breast Cancer Society, Inc.." Breast

Cancer Awareness Information, Support & Merchandise I
Breast Cancer Society, Inc.. N.p., n.d. Web. 9 June
2011. <http://www.breastcancersociety.org/aboutbreastcancer/
thebreastcancermovement/breastcancerpink.shtml>.

2. Claybourn, Joshua . " An Orange St. Patricks Day? - In The Agora."
In The Agora - current events, culture, faith, science and more.
N.p., 16 Mar. 2009. Web. 9 June 2011. <http://www.intheagora.
com/archives/2009/03/an-orange-st-patricks-day/>.

3. Green, Samantha. "History and Meaning of Gerbera Daisies."
Flowers Delivered - Send   Flowers Online, ProFlowers Flower
Delivery. N.p., n.d. Web. 9 June 2011. <http://www.proflowers.
com/flowerguide/flowermeanings/daisy-meanings.aspx>.

4. "Human Trafficking of Children in the United States." U.S.
Department of Education Office of Safe and Drug-Free Schools.
N.p., n.d. Web. 9 June 2011. <www2.ed.gov/about/offices/list/
osdfs/factsheet.html>.

5. "Statistics." National Center For Missing and Exploited Children. N.p.,
n.d. Web. 9 June 2011. <www.missingkids.com/missingkids/
servlet/PageServlet?LanguageCountry=en_US&PageId=2810#1 >.

6. Allen, Ernie. "Ernie Allen Human Trafficking Briefing for the
Congressional Victims Rights Caucus and Congressional
Human Trafficking Caucus." National Center for Missing and
Exploited Children. N.p., 21 July 2009. Web. 9 June 2011.
<http://www.missingkids.com/missingkids/servlet/NewsEventServ
let?LanguageCountry=en_US&PageId=4079>.

7. "Prostituted Youth - Domestic Violence & Sexual Assault Prevention -
Seattle Human Services   Department." Seattle.gov Home
Page - The Official Web Site for the City of Seattle,
Washington. N.p., n.d. Web. 9 June 2011. <http://www.seattle.
gov/humanservices/domesticviolence/prostitutedyouth/
nationalperspective.htm>.

8. "United States Senator Dianne Feinstein, California : News Room."
United States Senator Dianne Feinstein, California : Home. N.p.,
22 Dec. 2009. Web. 9 June 2011. <http://feinstein.
senate.gov/public/index.cfm?FuseAction=NewsRoom.

PressReleases&ContentRecord_id=b8a4b956-5056-8059-760a-4eb9130f8b7c&Region_id=&Issue_id=>.

Conclusion

1. Zollman, Peter. "Craigslist sex-for-sale ads may not return" but prostitution ads won't go away, either I AIMGroup.com." AIM Group - Interactive media and classified advertising consultants. N.p., 5 Sept. 2010. Web. 9 June 2011. <http://aimgroup.com/blog/2010/09/05/craigslist-sex-for-sale-ads-may-not-return-but-prostitution-ads-wont-go-away-either/>.

2. "Did You Know?." eyeheartworld.org. N.p., n.d. Web. 20 June 2011. <www.eyeheartworld.org/stats.php>.

3. "Penny (United States Coin)." Penny (United States Coin). N.p., n.d. Web. 9 June 2011. <penny-united-states-coin.co.tv/>.

4. "The United States Mint · About The Mint." The United States Mint. N.p., n.d. Web. 9 June 2011. <http://www.usmint.gov/about_the_mint/fun_facts/?action=fun_facts2>.

MAKE A DIFFERENCE

1. RAISE YOUR LEVEL OF AWARENESS: Become informed so you can share what you know with those around you.

2. HOST AN EVENT IN YOUR COMMUNITY: 5K run/ walk, Dinner and a Movie, banquet, motorcycle freedom ride or sports tournaments.

3. OUTREACH IN A RED LIGHT DISTRICT: Join an experienced group in your community, get training, be consistent, build relationships, and expect a rescue.

4. REFUSE TO CLICK: It only takes one click on any pornography website for another girl to be demanded as more supply. Don't do it and help save a potential victim.

5. TEACH CHILDREN ABOUT INTERNET SAFETY: Social media networks are a veil for predators to lure children.

6. SPEAK TO LOCAL LEGISLATORS: Call your governor, mayor, congressman, and senator to ask what they are doing to fight against Sex Slavery in your community.

7. BECOME A VOLUNTEER: Find out how you can help organizations that are fighting against Sex Slavery in your area. Central Florida residents can go to runforfreedom.net to complete a volunteer form.

8. JOIN THE ORANGE ARMY: Proclaim freedom by wearing Orange and telling everyone about your stand against Sex Slavery.

9. PARTNER WITH RUN FOR FREEDOM: Help us in our fight against Sex Slavery by becoming a financial support partner at runforfreedom.net.

10. PRAY: For victims to be freed, for many others to rise up and make a difference and for Sex Slavery to be eradicated in America.

YOU CAN MAKE A HUGE DIFFERENCE IN THE FIGHT AGAINST SEX SLAVERY!

HOW TO SPOT A VICTIM

You can stop Sex Slavery by becoming aware of some potential indicators. The following list will help you identify a victim who is caught in the sex trade:

A GIRL WHO...

... has inconsistencies in her stories
... has a controlling and/or abusive boyfriend
... has a tattoo signifying she belongs to someone
... has signs of physical abuse
... has several condoms and/or lubricants in her purse
... has one or more hotel keys
... has excessive amounts of cash on her
... has no identification or a false one
... has an inability to make eye contact
... is being watched from a distance by someone
... is seen hanging around hotel rooms
... lies about her age
... seems fearful, nervous, and/or depressed
... can't tell you where she bought her clothes
... dresses provocatively and much older than her age
... sounds scripted in her communication

If you suspect a possible victim, call the
24 hour Human Trafficking Hotline:

1-888-3737-888

For information about our Dream Home email:

info@runforfreedom.net

To report immediate danger call: 911

SPONSOR A GIRL FOR 1 YEAR AT A DOLLAR A DAY!

This program is designed to provide assistance to underwrite the cost of caring for a student. This payment will be $30 each month for a year or a one-time $360 contribution.

Please make checks payable to "Run for Freedom" and mail to P.O. Box 121122, Clermont, FL 34712 or go to **www.runforfreedom.net** to start a recurring payment on our donation page.

Thank you and God bless!

JOIN THE ORANGE CAMPAIGN!

Fight Sex Slavery By Wearing ORANGE!

Orange is the color for FREEDOM! By wearing orange you can proclaim freedom for victims and help us raise awareness about Sex Slavery in America. Help us get closer to our goal of launching a national "ORANGE CAMPAIGN" in America and making Orange for Freedom as well known as Pink is to Breast Cancer Cure.

All proceeds from the FREEDOM STORE go to Run for Freedom, to allow us to operate our Dream Home for rescued victims of Sex Slavery. Not only are you donating, but you are enlisting in the army that is fighting the fight against Sex Slavery.

WWW.RUNFORFREEDOMSTORE.NET